Research for Better Teaching is a group of ten educators each of whom works individually with six to ten school districts per year. We offer courses in year-long and intensive week formats as well as follow-up modules. These courses focus on four separate areas: the study of teaching, supervision and evaluation, the school as an organization and special projects and services.

Our objective is to help school districts make the study of teaching an ongoing and permanent part of professional life, managed by the districts themselves.

We work to:

- expand staff understanding of the extensive knowledge base about teaching and its practical application in the classroom;

- improve administrators' individual skills and system-wide structures for conducting supervision and evaluation; *and*

- strengthen the school as an organization.

ACKNOWLEDGEMENTS

I wish to thank the many educators over the years who have helped develop the ideas in this monograph through their challenges, their commitment to good practice, and their willingness to share with me the hard practical work of improving supervision and evaluation in their districts.

David Horton, principal of the Estabrook School in Lexington, Massachusetts asked a key question in 1984 which marked a turning point in developing the Claims/ Evidence/Interpretations/Judgments framework for writing classroom observations that is so central to this piece. Lois Keiger and Karen Lane of the Concord Teachers Association proposed a procedure in their contract for dealing with less than satisfactory teaching that became a model for much of RBT's later work in shaping evaluation systems. Irwin Blumer, Carolee Matsumoto, Dick Sederstrom, and Tom Scott in Concord, Massachusetts showed what could be done with rigorous evaluation of evaluators and commitment to long term training and support of administrators.

Louise Thompson, Director of Training at RBT, helped several New England and Midwest districts implement the model in this monograph through superb training and follow up consulting. Louise, Peggy McMullen, Paula Rutherford, Andy Platt, and Kim Marshall gave excellent feedback and suggestions for changes to earlier versions of this manuscript. Peggy and Maria Storm in particular provided insights into the structure of the monograph that greatly increased its clarity.

Leon Levesque and Stan Sawyer from The River Valley School District and John True and Paul Dulac from S.A.D. 48 in New Hampshire were generous in letting us reprint much of their teacher evaluation handbooks in Appendix D.

Marilyn Brannigan and a dedicated committee of administrators and teachers in Chappaqua, N.Y. did a magnificent job over a one-year period of developing and implementing a multiple year professional growth cycle that not only carried out the model in Chapter IV with fidelity, but was a model of inclusive and legitimate decision-making. This model still thrives six years later.

Each of the thousands of educators I have worked with on this topic in their own districts, schools, and departments over the last twelve years has contributed to the ever increasing clarity of the knowledge base on doing supervision and evaluation well. I am grateful to them all and consider this work the fruit of collaborative struggle and learning together.

TABLE OF CONTENTS

Appendices

I.
Introduction

INTRODUCTION

The children were working busily at their desks. Ben, their teacher, was leaning over a boy and in his calm, solicitous way, coaching him through a math problem. I noticed a 4th grader from another section come quietly through the door and hand Ben a note. Ben read it, smiled, and laid it on his desk for me to see as he went off to tend to other children.

"Fred has his pad," it said. The note was unsigned but was obviously from Marsha, the teacher of another 4th grade on the other side of the building. Both Ben and I knew the meaning of that cryptic message, as I imagine any teacher in the school would. Fred was the principal and this morning he was visiting classrooms to do evaluations.

This incident has stuck with me for many years as one of those vivid images that crystallize the complicated meanings of events to people in institutions. That note was a warning, a favor, a joke all at the same time; it was also a symbol of the significance of evaluation in the lives of these teachers and more poignantly, a gesture that signified the gap between what teacher evaluation could be and what it typically is. Here was a good principal who was a skilled and positive observer doing his administrative duty in a school that had a very positive climate. Yet the anticipation of that event by Marsha, who sent the note, and Ben, who received it, was one of wry but defensive preparation despite the fact that they were both excellent teachers and recognized as such. Wry but defensive preparation, as if to say, "Here's another one to get through." Such had been my reaction to evaluation as a teacher in previous years too; and so, I wager, is that of most teachers in the United States on such occasions.

While quite understandable and human, this event and all the feelings it captures should motivate us to rethink the purpose and outcomes of teacher evaluation and its impact on school culture. *How can we use teacher evaluation as a positive force to strengthen school culture?* No single practice has more capacity for strengthening or weakening that culture, or more powerfully condenses the way teachers experience the cultural norms of their school, than evaluation.

At Research for Better Teaching, we have learned a great deal about supervision and evaluation in working with schools over the last decade. One of the most important lessons has been that *how* we do supervision and evaluation sends powerful messages to the staff and community about whether or not we believe teaching is important, whether or not we believe teachers are decision-makers, and whether or not we believe teachers must be constant learners. The answer to all three questions, of course, should be "Yes!" In fact, the improvement of schools depends on it being yes. Thus the structure of supervision and evaluation and the knowledge and skills of those who deliver them become critical variables in making schools satisfying, growth-oriented environments for adults, places where adults feel good, work hard and believe they can make a difference for students.

The purpose of this monograph is to examine those factors which make supervision and evaluation "really work," that is, contribute to the larger purpose of building an environment where educators can deliver their best and children can learn the most. In the sections that follow, all of our recommendations are made in light of this larger purpose and with an underlying awareness of the larger "system" of school improvement through strong organizational culture.

II.
Defining
the Problem

DEFINING THE PROBLEM

Our goal in writing this monograph—and yours, we trust, in reading it—is to answer the question, "What does it take to make supervision and evaluation really work?" Perhaps we should start by asking how we would know if they were?

Saying we want to "improve instruction" is axiomatic but also not very illuminating. Supervision and evaluation are becoming words of marginal utility in our business because of the confusing and conflicting meanings behind these terms. Let's start afresh, temporarily holding the two terms in abeyance, and take another look at both the structure and function of what we do as evaluators.

The activity we are really talking about here is the *observation of teaching*. We want many different but equally important outcomes from this observation. What follows is a list of nine such outcomes *all* of which we would be able to accomplish if supervision and evaluation were really working. They are, in effect, the criteria against which to measure our success.

Nine Functions of Observation

Cheerleading

For one thing, we want teachers who are doing a good job to get *believable feedback* to that effect. We want such people to feel *recognized, validated and reinforced* in the specifics of how and why their effective practices are effective, how and why their skillful performances are skillful.

Facilitating

For another, we want teachers to have someone knowledgeable about the education business and with good facilitation skills to help them think through personal, professional goals and how to meet them. This outcome has to do with *helping teachers articulate and meet their own agendas*.

Stimulating

We want teachers to get stimulating insights and *suggestions for alternative or new techniques* to use in their teaching, not because they are doing anything wrong, but just to help them stretch and grow. This outcome has to do with using outside input and other eyes to broaden teachers' thinking.

Problem Solving

We want teachers to have someone to *help them gather data and think through solutions to problems* they are working on—perhaps problems concerning students or curriculum or instructional technique. Perhaps the best help may be articulating exactly what the problem really *is*.

Monitoring

We want to be sure the curriculum we claim to be delivering is really being delivered. Thus we want some systematic form of observation across teachers to *monitor the fidelity of curriculum* delivered in relation to district and school commitments. Further, we want to be able to intervene with corrective feedback when we find discrepancies between individual teacher performances and important district curriculum commitments.[1]

Directing

We want to be able to *identify weak areas* in teachers' repertoires and be able to *focus teachers on specific steps for improvement*.

Making Decisions

We want to have *valid and reliable data for making decisions* about such things as hiring, grade assignment, school transfers, granting of tenure, commendations, promotions and appointments.

Remediating and Dismissing

We want to be able to *identify teachers who are functioning at an unsatisfactory level* overall and directly intervene to either remediate successfully or dismiss.

Finally, there is an outcome for observation that is more abstract than the previous eight, but in a way is an umbrella over them all:

Valuing Teaching as a Profession

Real observation and quality feedback takes time and energy. To deliver it says that *teaching is important,* that it makes a difference. It advances the value that out of all the important things in a school, nothing is more important than what goes on between teachers and students every day, class to class, minute to minute. This is a strong message of respect to teachers and must be part of any effort to elevate the profession.

---

[1] Curriculum monitoring is more systematic when augmented by review of lesson plans and collected drafts of tests and student project assignments.

Defining Supervision and Evaluation

What we have now is a list of nine functions for observation or put another way, nine outcomes we would like to see as a result of the way we do observation in a given school or district.

We would have no need, by the way, to use the terms "supervision" or "evaluation" in order to discuss the next logical question, which is: how can we arrange to have observation attain the above nine outcomes? Nevertheless, since the terms will probably not be disappearing from the professional scene in the near future, we would like to suggest a useful way to define them.

Let "supervision" mean the first four outcomes: Cheerleading, Facilitating, Stimulating and Problem Solving. Let "evaluation" mean the next four outcomes: Monitoring, Directing, Making Decisions and Remediating and Dismissing. *The boundary line between supervision and evaluation comes when the observer is making decisions with the information from the observation.* All eight activities do involve observing teachers; all eight involve talking to them about what we have seen; and all eight can involve writing about it. But only 5-8 involve making decisions from a position of authority that affect the teachers' working conditions (and perhaps job status). Figure 2.1 summarizes this division of outcomes.

By grouping our observation outcomes in this manner, we can then further condense our objectives into the following two statements:

1) We want our system for observing teachers to give them *frequent, high quality feedback* on their practice from *someone who knows what he/she is talking about.* (Cheerleading, Facilitating, Stimulating, Problem Solving)

2) We want our system for observing teachers to produce judgments about the performance level and job status of teachers, and most importantly, whether or not they are performing up to district standards. (Monitoring, Directing, Assigning, Remediating and Dismissing)

Let us clarify a few of the above terms. "High-quality feedback" means objective information about practice that is useful to teachers in stretching their thinking, helping them reflect on a problem or goal on which they are working or focusing them on something new. "Frequent" means about six times a year.[1] Maybe we can't provide this every year for every professional; but we should aim for it at least every few years. And *something,* even if not of this intensity, needs to happen *every* year to focus teachers on examining their teaching.

---

[1] Six is an arbitrary number. There is nothing sacred about it; it is just that in our experience, frequency of contact, frequency of observation, significantly in excess of the two or three observations provided by most evaluation systems today is needed to accustom teachers to more public discourse about their practice and to produce truly useful analysis and feedback for them.

FIGURE 2-1

What do we want our systems for observing teachers to accomplish?

SUPERVISION	1.	Cheerleading	validating teachers' effectiveness in a believable and strength-building way
	2.	Facilitating	helping teachers think about and plan to meet self-set goals
	3.	Stimulating	stretching teachers' thinking about their instructional decisions
	4.	Problem Solving	facilitating teachers' analyzing and solving classroom problems

The boundary between supervision and evaluation comes when the observer is **making decisions** with the information from the observation.

EVALUATION	5.	Monitoring	monitoring for fidelity of curriculum implementation
	6.	Directing	directing teachers to weak areas in their teaching and helping them improve
	7.	Making Decisions	about teacher placement, hiring, commendation, promotion, tenure
	8.	Remediating/ Dismissing	identifying incompetent teachers and dealing with them (remediation, counselling out, dismissal)
VALUING	9.	Valuing the Profession	confirming the paramount importance of good teaching

? nonsense decisions in 1-4 as well?

"Someone who knows what they are talking about" means, in the case of teachers, someone who is knowledgeable about teaching, good at observing, skillful at analyzing and properly tuned to the teacher's need for information, stimulation, or direction (whichever is appropriate).

Making Evaluation Work

Now let's focus on the second issue mentioned above—producing judgments about whether a teacher's performance is up to district standards. What is important is that teachers who do not meet district standards be identified, notified and worked with intensively. Through fair and comprehensive procedures, they either improve significantly or are dismissed.

We find it paradoxical to be addressing inadequate teaching first in this chapter. The other outcome for observation that we listed is the more significant in the long term, that is, arranging for frequent, high quality feedback to teachers. But our learning from experience in school districts has been that we cannot wade right in to increase observational feedback to maximum effect without getting "evaluation" squared away first.

We have learned in school districts over and over again that healthy cultural conditions, energized growth-oriented workplaces for adults and the practices that support them, cannot flourish at their highest level unless procedures for "at-risk" teachers and "dismissal" actions are clearly developed, are operating successfully and fairly and are seen by teachers as 1) maintaining worthwhile professional standards and 2) not threatening or even applicable to the vast majority of practitioners.

Let's put it another way: until we get the guts and the skills to dismiss incompetents and remediate unsatisfactory performers with clear procedures and do so consistently, we severely limit our chances of launching healthy collegial practices that will result in sustained teacher growth and become a permanent part of institutional life. Perhaps strong, fair evaluation gives administrators respect and credibility on which they can later draw as they start to build a strong school culture based on collaboration and risk taking. Whatever the explanation, it seems that even though establishing conditions for continued professional growth is our higher goal, we can't get there unless we deal with the unpleasant stuff first.

Thus in the list of nine tasks below, readers will note significant attention to the "unpleasant stuff" of judgment and dismissal—not because that is our goal, but because we know it must be gotten through intelligently, courageously and clearly on our way to the other goals of observation. With that context in mind, here are nine tasks we have learned lead to supervision and evaluation that will work on all counts.

1. Development of a *common language and concept system* for talking about teaching.

2. Development of criteria for effective teaching that are published, understood by all and part of the enculturation process of all newly hired personnel.

3. School system commitment to improving supervision and evaluation as a multiple year goal, buttressed by systematic *evaluation of the evaluators* on their ability to evaluate (the ultimate signal that something is important).

4. Multiple-year in-depth *skill training for administrators* in the knowledge base about teaching, taking observation notes swiftly, selectively and accurately; writing with a balance of claims, evidence, interpretations, judgments and suggestions; writing clearly and concisely; developing skills for conferring with teachers at different levels of personal and professional development from well-developed, autonomous decision makers to low-performing people to whom significant negative information must be delivered.

5. "At-risk" and "dismissal" procedures that are fair, forthright, humane, clearly signalled and clearly different from the purposes of observation at other times.

6. Evaluation that "counts," insulated from supervision for improvement by separate procedures and calendar periods (though not necessarily by different personnel).

7. Systematic induction and training of newly-hired administrators and teachers.

8. Development of structures, resources and cultural expectations that support teachers getting frequent, quality feedback on their practice from a knowledgeable professional.

9. Development of structures, resources and cultural expectations that support teachers and administrators viewing themselves as constant learners.

These nine tasks provide the essential building blocks of effective supervision and evaluation; once in place they will provide a solid foundation upon which to build a school culture that truly encourages learning for staff and students alike. In the chapters that follow, we will share what we have learned about accomplishing each of these tasks effectively.

III.
The Building Blocks of Supervision and Evaluation

THE BUILDING BLOCKS
OF SUPERVISION AND EVALUATION

Before examining specific tools of supervision and evaluation such as procedures and forms, we need to make sure that a vital foundation is in place. Without understanding and agreement on these basic building blocks, the best procedures and forms in the world will be erratically implemented and opportunities will be lost to make supervision and evaluation strengthen the school as an organization.

Common Language and Concept System

All true professions have a distinct vocabulary that draws on a disciplined body of knowledge. Phil Schlecty (1986) points out that a disciplined body of knowledge is not the same—nor need it be—as a scientific body of knowledge. The legal profession does not have a scientific knowledge base, but it most certainly does have a disciplined one. Likewise, we in education have a disciplined body of knowledge upon which to base a professional language. Without overindulging in jargon-making, we must familiarize ourselves with the truly immense and valuable knowledge base about teaching that has developed rapidly over the past three decades of observational studies.

Becoming conversant in our own professional language is an essential step in achieving the desirable outcomes we have previously set as the goals of observation. Having a *common language and concept system for talking about teaching* is essential if professionals are going to communicate meaningfully about what is going on in classrooms. There must be common concepts about what the important zones of performance are in which all teachers act. Another way of posing this issue is to ask what tasks do teachers have in common, the performance of which bears on student learning (e.g., communicating challenging but appropriate academic expectations to students; presenting and explaining new material clearly and effectively; building relations of regard and respect with students). There must be terms—a professional vocabulary—for describing not only these important performance areas but also the repertoire of legitimate techniques available for accomplishing our teaching objectives.[1] (See Appendix C, Parameters Summary.)

---

[1] One good place to start developing a common language and concept system is *The Skillful Teacher* (Saphier and Gower, 1987) which examines the rich knowledge base about classroom instruction skills and the range of teaching strategies available for accomplishing individual instructional tasks.

Criteria for Effective Teaching

Another important step in the development of a good evaluation system is the establishment and system-wide adoption of agreed upon criteria for effective teaching. Early in the process of developing a teacher evaluation system, a representative committee of school people needs to come up with from five to ten areas of performance that they value in effective teaching. This effort provides school systems with the opportunity to pull together their various constituencies—parents, students, teachers and administrators—and come to a consensus over their understanding of "good teaching." The resulting "Criteria for Effective Teaching" becomes the keystone of everything that comes later. It becomes important *not as a checklist* but as a much broader value statement representing the school district's image of what should be happening for students. (See Appendix A for sample "Criteria for Effective Teaching".)

The "Criteria for Effective Teaching" next must become incorporated into evaluation procedures. A good evaluation system embodies a clear position about what the district thinks is most important in a teacher's performance, that is, what the district values and expects a person to do in teachers' multiple roles. For example, if one of the value commitments of the school district is "Respect for Human Differences," as it is in one of the districts where we work, then it should be one of the areas addressed in the narrative evaluation instrument and actually appear on the form as a numbered heading.

The broad-based involvement of staff in the development of "Criteria for Effective Teaching" is important, if we expect evaluation to be seen as legitimate and if we expect to hold staff accountable for performance. Just the process of creating a good evaluation system based on effective teaching criteria can become a professional development activity for those who participate from within the school system as well as a foundation for productive dialogue on teaching for everyone within the community.

Multi-year In-depth Skill Training for Administrators

The next task required to make supervision and evaluation really work is multi-year, in-depth skill training for administrators. The point we would like to emphasize is "multi-year." Few principals have systematic training in classroom observation behind them when selected for the job, and few ever get it later. Furthermore, no single course is going to give an individual all the skills he or she needs. Yet, this training is so important, so central a part of the principal's role, that it must be given high priority (as opposed to no priority now in most districts, judging by the amount of professional development time given to administrators for classroom observation skills).

Ample materials are available for this kind of training. One starting point is the knowledge base about teaching mentioned earlier (Saphier and Gower, 1987). Administrators need to learn with academic rigor the essential concepts from the knowledge base and then practice looking for and recording in good notes occurrences of important teaching behaviors.

In our courses we find it highly useful to couple studying the concepts from the knowledge base on teaching with looking at carefully selected video clips of live teaching. Observers also need to learn and practice note-taking skills that enable them to capture literally accurate renderings of quotes and visible events, yet not become so buried in writing that they lose visual contact with the class.

Writing skills should be part of the training too. Improving writing skills with respect to direct language and elimination of needless words would probably benefit all of us, but writing about teaching benefits particularly from a format that balances claims, evidence, interpretations and judgments. A detailed description of writing in this format is presented on pages 39-40 and examples of products are in Appendix B, "Sample Classroom Observation Write-Ups."

The training described above usually puts administrators in the position of noticing more clearly teachers' many strengths and being able to be more convincing in remarking on these strengths. Second, it puts administrators in a better position to spread the good ideas and techniques they have gleaned from their training to the teachers they observe because they are more analytical and articulate now about what they see. Third, it puts them in a position, often for the first time, of really noticing an individual's ineffective teaching and being able to isolate in behavior what the problems are.

Thus one outcome of this training is that it puts many administrators in the position of being able to confront ineffective teaching effectively! And that, in turn, puts them in the difficult position of having to deliver significant negative information to a very small number of people...but perhaps people they have known and had on staff for many years. This stressful situation calls for specific training and support for administrators around this vital part of their job, a task nobody likes, but no one else can do. And doing it well is one important element in making supervision and evaluation really work.[1]

---

[1]Though this monograph is not the place to expand on the topic of how to deliver negative information, it is interesting to note that in many districts where we have done training as described above, a demand has been created for work on conferencing in these situations. A subsequent monograph will address the topic thoroughly.

Systematic Induction and Training of New Personnel
(Both Administrators and Teachers)

The study of teaching should also be a required part of both administrators' and teachers' first year or two in the district. Teaching and learning and what goes on between teachers and students day-to-day and class-to-class is the most important part of our business. Our induction procedures for all new personnel should signal this value if we believe it. Furthermore, the requirement that everyone participate in this training carries with it the implication that ongoing professional development is a district mission for administrators and teachers alike.

In several districts where we work as consultants, all newly-hired teachers are required to take a course sometime in their first two years on the knowledge base on teaching. The purpose of this course is to stimulate collegiality and experimentation. It is *not* a training course in the district's preferred model of teaching, but rather an exploration of the rich knowledge base of the craft. The course puts people in peer groups and structures peer observation for all participants. (See the section on peer observation in Chapter V.) Seasoned teachers new to the district and novices alike engage in an experience based on the notion that no one knows everything about teaching and everyone has more to learn from the knowledge base and from each other. This kind of course is a district culture builder; it is the kind of thing a district can do to strengthen cultural elements district-wide.

Effective At-risk and Dismissal Procedures

At the other end of the spectrum, but equally important, are at-risk and dismissal procedures. While these procedures pertain to only a very small number of people, they have a very large impact on school culture. They must be—and be seen as—*prompt, fair, humane* and *decisive:*

— *prompt* in that teaching problems are not allowed to slide since children are losing daily when teachers are doing a poor job;

— *fair* in that teachers subject to these procedures have every chance to improve and significant genuine energy goes into helping them do so;

— *humane* in that teachers' feelings are recognized and support is offered, sometimes including job counselling and professional time with a career consultant to find a suitable and satisfying position; and

— *decisive* in that administrators become serious about inadequate teaching and cases are resolved with either clear improvement or termination of teaching.

At-risk and dismissal procedures can be very hard to initiate when the teacher concerned:

a) has received positive evaluations from previous evaluators who are less conscientious or less aware,

b) is a nice person or a friend or both,

c) will become upset about being harassed and perhaps invoke legalistic prerogatives,

d) is popular with faculty and will get much support making the administrator feel isolated, or

e-z) any number of other unpleasant possibilities you as readers can probably anticipate (and may have experienced).

Such factors have discouraged many administrators and sometimes whole districts from confronting the need for honest evaluation. In such places we see coping strategies such as the "Dance of the Lemons" in which a few inadequate teachers are passed from school to school, dallying one or two years at each before the principal passes the person along to the next unsuspecting site. This practice has negative effects on district morale and on relations between principals, to say nothing of the children who are consistently losing. With the skills and procedures described in this monograph, plus a little dose of courage and mutual support among administrators, this syndrome can be stopped dead in its tracks.

Separate Procedures for Unsatisfactory Teaching

Even though we oppose rating and ranking teachers (see p. 45), there is *one* rating that should be given explicitly, if necessary, but only in the final evaluation form. This rating is "less-than-satisfactory" or words to that effect. Whatever phrase is picked, it must mean that overall the teacher's performance is not up to district standards. In other words, it is bad enough so that if it stays at this level, dismissal will follow. Along the curve of performance there are not many teachers in this category, but they need to be identified explicitly, told they are in that category and informed regarding the special help and evaluation procedures they will be entering. In this section we will get into some detail about how this can be done successfully.

Dismissal procedures for teachers who do not improve usually take two years. During year one, the evaluator does frequent observations, more than the standard two or three, because of concerns that are becoming apparent. The principal or department chair, after several observations and conferences with the teacher, concludes that improvement is not taking place. He/she therefore meets with the superintendent and personnel director. They review all the documentation and decide whether or not to place the teacher in the "less than satisfactory" category for the coming year. By March of the first year, the teacher receives a letter from the superintendent to that effect. The special procedures that will operate are outlined in the letter. They include two, preferably three, observers: the principal and perhaps two other principals for elementary teachers; perhaps two principals and a department head for secondary teachers. The procedure includes bi-weekly observations and write-ups by the three evaluators rotating in sequence. Though all three write their observations, one person remains the primary supervisor and organizer of feedback for the teacher.

In addition, a remediation plan is built using resources of the district to provide in-classroom help to the "less-than-satisfactory" teacher. Genuine and extensive effort is exerted to help the teacher improve and may also include help with planning lessons as well as interactive teaching. These efforts are mobilized during the spring of year one and implemented immediately. Those directly helping the teacher do not write evaluations.

By February of year two, the three observers have made a substantial number of observations and write-ups—probably about four each. They then sit down for an afternoon and, by going over all the observations done to date, decide if the teacher has improved enough to move out of the "less-than-satisfactory" category. In our experience, about half such teachers do, suggesting they needed either the push, the feedback and help, or the attention to really start working on their own teaching (perhaps all three). The three evaluators together write a final summary evaluation for the teacher, ending with a declaration of the teacher's status (still "less-than-satisfactory" or removed from that category). Those who do not improve enough are notified formally by this final evaluation report which is usually jointly written by the three observers in March. If insufficient progress has been made, dismissal proceedings are now brought before the board.

What is important about this process is that it be clearly different from what all the other teachers experience, that the reasons for that difference be clear to everybody in the district and that both the approach and labeling of a teacher as "less-than-satisfactory" be clearly signalled. The March letter in year one of the procedures we recommended is the signal. (There could certainly be other forms of delivering that message and initiating the intensive procedures.)

The negotiated contract between teachers union and school board must at least allow and at best specifically include and describe the "less-than-satisfactory" procedures and schedule of activities for teachers so labeled.

Meanwhile other teachers *not* in the "less-than-satisfactory" category (practically everybody) need to know when a judgment is made about them and be given a document that says so. This should be called a Final Evaluation Summary and need not be done every year. Every three or four years would be sufficient.

What we are proposing, and what currently operates in a number of districts where we work, is a cycle of activities where *formal evaluation* only happens once every three or four years—meaning *observation for the purpose of certifying the teacher as okay.* "Okay" means meeting district standards, *not* "less-than-satisfactory." It is like one's annual health check-up (in this case, tri-annual). We are not looking to rate people for their relative robustness, but rather to catch any maladies and deal with them. This is how we should define evaluation—make it clearly judgmental for purposes of meeting minimal standards and nothing else. Two or three observations and a final evaluation summary will do the job. (See discussion of Multiple Year Evaluation Cycles, Chapter V.)

And, of course, anytime there is serious concern about a teacher for some reason they can be "evaluated" out of cycle.

Evaluating the Evaluators

The significant decision-makers of a district, including school board and superintendent, must show by word and deed that their commitment to improving the evaluation process is real. This means using the district-wide goal setting process annually, if they have one, to reiterate their goals and plan the next steps; it means committing time, money and training resources to their goals, and in the case of evaluation, it means formally evaluating the evaluators on their ability to evaluate!

In the districts where our work has had the most impact, the person or persons who directly supervise evaluators have taken all the training and then visited evaluators on-site frequently (an average of once a month). This means, for example, superintendents visiting principals, asking to see their written observations of teachers and critiquing their writing. It might also mean a high school principal visiting department chairs, or a sub-district superintendent visiting principals and asking to do an observation with them, then comparing notes and discussing their analysis of the teaching and approach to the post-conference, or it might mean collecting observations. Without these strong signals, the message will not be received. Administrators, like anyone else, will pay serious attention to the things on which they themselves are evaluated.

In this chapter we have described building blocks for supervision and evaluation that really work:

- common language and concept system,

- criteria for effective teaching,

- multi-year in-depth training for administrators,

- systematic induction and training of new personnel,

- effective at-risk and dismissal procedures,

- separate procedures for unsatisfactory teaching, and

- evaluating the evaluators.

These building blocks represent long-term commitments to certain kinds of training and enculturation of new people and also commitments to tenacity, clarity and thoroughness in dealing with unsatisfactory teaching. In the next chapter we look inside the implementation of good evaluation at the specific nuts and bolts of procedures and forms.

IV.
The Tools of
Evaluation

THE TOOLS OF EVALUATION

Form influences substance in any area of human affairs, and it is no different in the very human domain of evaluating performance. We have learned that certain forms and procedures greatly facilitate carrying out the principles we have described in previous chapters. A summary of them follows.

Narrative Observation Reports

All written reports of classroom observations should be narrative. *The best form is a blank sheet of paper.* Checklists are seductive because they are easy and quick but they suffer from several fatal flaws: first they never seem to include enough categories, that is, an observer will often witness an event of some significance to learning that doesn't fit into one of the categories. The more categories there are, the more likely this is to happen, since the categories become rather specific. Second, there is no place on the form to record evidence or supporting data for the evaluator's claim. Figure 4-1 shows a form that suffers from these two shortcomings.

Third, a checklist requires the observer either to check the presence of a certain behavior or give the teacher some sort of quality rating on the item. The first is useless, and the second is usually uninformative at best and destructive at worst. Knowing the presence or absence of a certain behavior is useless unless we know how it was used, in what context…in other words if the behavior was used *appropriately.*

"Praise" is a good example. In the 60s and 70s (and beyond) praise appeared as a checklist item on many evaluation instruments. Teachers received "credit" and were positively evaluated if observers noted incidences of praise to students. Yet by 1979 it was clear (Brophy, 1979) that what mattered about praise was *how* it was given and how it was *perceived.* Effective praise needed to be specific, contingent on being really deserved, genuinely delivered in language appropriate to the child's culture and varied. Furthermore, even these features didn't guarantee effectiveness since the child might perceive the praise as, for example, an unwelcome spotlight (if publicly given) or a manipulative move to get him to do something the teacher wanted.

Finally, they induce teachers to add up their "scores"—how many "excellents," how many "goods," how many "satisfactories." Thus they divert attention from substance and direct it to one's "grades."

In between narratives and checklists are observation forms that have several categories related to teacher performance listed on the form with a few inches of white space underneath. Figures 4-2 and 4-3 are examples of this type of observation form.

These forms are better than checklists but suffer two of their drawbacks. First, the white space limits the amount an observer can write about a given category. One can always attach addenda, but that is cumbersome. Moreover, the structure and layout of these forms suggest each category should be filled in, even if it is not relevant to the class observed. These flaws could be remedied by:

a) making the categories few enough and broad enough to cover all possible teaching/learning events,

b) summarizing them in several lines at the head of the form so they are still mentioned, still present to remind observer and teacher they are important, but do not limit, either directly or by implication, how much an observer writes about a given part of a class, and

c) making the rest of the form after this heading just blank paper.

An alternative to the short list of criteria in the heading is to have a background document that lists what the district considers important in teaching and states that these are the kind of things for which observers will be looking. The "Criteria of Effective Teaching" discussed earlier is a good source for developing this list. (See Appendix A.) A recommended observation form itself follows in Figure 4-4.

We offer one additional argument against checklists and instruments with categories: they efface a reader's sense of the flow of the class—the way events unfolded. This results from organizing events by category rather than by chronology. Chronological narratives enable not only the sequence of events to be presented, but also their relation to one another; sometimes (not always) this is an important option to have for describing important classroom events. Examples of such narrative write-ups are provided in Appendix B.

FIGURE 4-1

Negative Example 1

Total No. of Visits _____
Total No. of Hours _____

PUBLIC SCHOOLS

COMPREHENSIVE _____
SUPPLEMENTARY _____

EVALUATION FORM
Refer to Evaluation Instrument

Teacher _____ School _____

Date _____ Evaluator _____ Position _____

Grade or subject _____ Present Status (Tenure, etc.) _____

> Use: **S** - Superior, **C** - Competent, **N** - Needs Improvement, to mark each item. Items that have
> not been observed during visits or which do not apply should be left unmarked.

PERSONAL CHARACTERISTICS

_____   1.   The teacher is fair, impartial and objective in treatment of pupils.

_____   2.   The teacher shows self-control.

_____   3.   The teacher is careful of voice and uses appropriate language.

_____   4.   The teacher contributes to group thinking of staff.

_____   5.   The teacher is prompt and dependable in the performance of duties.

_____   6.   The teacher willingly accepts and implements suggestions.

         7.   Comments (optional)

_____

_____

_____

_____

CLASSROOM PROCEDURES AND EFFECTIVENESS

_____   8.   Teacher shows mastery of subject matter.

_____   9.   Teacher adjusts the physical features of room to provide a healthful and attractive environment as far as circumstances permit.

_____   10.   Pupils are met in a friendly and empathetic manner.

_____   11.   Contributions and efforts of individual pupils and groups are given recognition.

_____   12.   Plans are adaptable and meet the different needs, learning rates and levels of pupils.

_____   13.   Pupils and teachers understand purpose of the lesson and engage in activities to fulfill this purpose.

_____   14.   Definite provision is made for repetition, review and recall of basic learnings.

_____   15.   Teacher provides classroom leadership and disciplines in a quiet, dignified and positive manner.

_____   16.   Teacher assists pupils in developing a sense of responsibility, self-discipline, cooperation and respect for others.

_____   17.   Teacher consistently assists pupils in appraising their own work.

_____   18.   Problems are presented in a manner which stimulates pupils to contribute to the solution.

_____   19.   The teacher employs a variety of materials and techniques appropriate to the varying abilities and backgrounds of the pupils.

_____   20.   Teacher guides the pupils into efficient study habits.

_____   21.   The teacher enriches the program by using available school and community resources and equipment.

The Tools of Evaluation

_____ 22. Teacher provides opportunities for creative work.

_____ 23. The teacher implements the curriculum of the _____ Public Schools.

_____ 24. The teacher encourages the pupils to effectively participate in classroom discussion activities.

_____ 25. The teacher consistently assesses the progress of each pupil.

_____ 26. The teacher encourages pupils to become independent learners and helps them to use appropriate materials for this objective.

27. Comments (optional)

_____

_____

_____

_____

PROFESSIONAL ATTITUDES AND ACTIVITIES

_____ 28. The teacher works cooperatively with school associates for the good of the school as a whole.

_____ 29. The teacher seeks and uses the advice and assistance of specialists to supplement his own teaching.

_____ 30. Teacher is impartial, constructive and cooperative in relations with parents.

_____ 31. The teacher shows a desire to grow in the profession by participating in appropriate professional activities.

_____ 32. The teacher displays critical interest in new ideas.

_____ 33. The teacher uses discretion and tact and supports the school's programs and policies in all contacts with the public.

34. Comments (optional)

_____

_____

_____

COMMENDATIONS: _____

_____

_____

_____

RECOMMENDATIONS: _____

_____

_____

_____

		Yes	No
1.	Should be appointed for a full year (If teacher has been here only a part of a school year)	_____	_____
2.	Should be given second appointment.	_____	_____
3.	Should be given a third appointment.	_____	_____
4.	Should be given a tenure appointment.	_____	_____
5.	Should be granted normal increment.	_____	_____

Evaluator's Signature:

Teacher's comments if desired:

_____

_____

_____

_____

_____

I have seen this evaluation form, a conference has been held with the evaluator and the stated number of visits and hours is correct.

Date of conference _____ Evaluated _____

FIGURE 4-2

Negative Example 2

PUBLIC SCHOOLS
TEACHER OBSERVATION REPORT

Date _____

Teacher _____ Observer _____

School _____ Grade _____ Class Size _____

Subject/Level_____

INSTRUCTIONS TO OBSERVER: Each area in the observation report must be rated using a check mark in the appropriate box. The symbols are BS=below standard; ES=expected standard; AS=above standard; O=outstanding. If the rating is "below standard" the observer must comment in the space provided.

A. PREPARATION — Plans are sufficiently detailed for lessons being taught and provide necessary information for substitute teachers.

COMMENT:

BS	ES	AS	O

B KNOWLEDGE OF SUBJECT — Teacher has a clear understanding of and enthusiasm for the subject and respects the level of ability of the students within the class.

COMMENT:

BS	ES	AS	O

C. EXECUTION OF LESSON — Lesson and materials are presented effectively through use of different teaching expression and effective questioning techniques.

COMMENT:

BS	ES	AS	O

D. STUDENT PARTICIPATION AND EVALUATION— Teacher allows for student questioning and input into the lesson, as well as sufficient homework, tests and other grades which are used to evaluate each student's performance. Effective records of students' performance are maintained for each class.

COMMENT:

BS	ES	AS	O

E. CLASSROOM MANAGEMENT— A stimulating learning environment is maintained with appropriate materials displayed and available to students. Teacher keeps accurate records of student attendance and uses good judgment in order to maintain effective classroom control.

COMMENT:

BS	ES	AS	O

The observer is required to make appropriate commendations and recommendations which are to be based on this classroom observation.

COMMENDATIONS:

RECOMMENDATIONS:

General Rating of Lesson Observation:

Below Standard ____   Expected Standard ____   Above Standard ____   Outstanding ____

_____   _____
Observer's Signature   Teacher's Signature

Teacher's Comments (optional)

FIGURE 4-3

Negative Example 3
PUBLIC SCHOOLS

TEACHER OBSERVATION REPORT
TENURED TEACHERS

Teacher's Name _____ Date_____

Subject/Level _____ Period _____

Specific topic, skill or activity being taught_____

_____

I. TEACHING EFFECTIVENESS

    1. Preparation and planning of lesson   5. Student interest and attention

    2. Knowledge of subject matter   6. Student participation and response

    3. Skill in presenting subject matter   7. Use of a variety of materials

    4. Explanation of new terms, concepts or processes   8. Attention to individual differences

                                            9. Care in making assignments

    Comments:_____

_____

_____

_____

_____

II. CLASSROOM MANAGEMENT

    1. Discipline — classroom control   4. Alertness and awareness with
                                                respect to student behavior

    2. Care of room (neatness/orderliness)   5. Attention to routine matters

                                              6. Attention to heating, lighting
    3. Effective use of time   and ventilation

    Comments:_____

_____

_____

_____

_____

_____

_____

_____

III. PERSONAL QUALITIES

1. General Appearance
2. Energy and Vitality
3. Command of English
4. Voice (volume and inflection)
5. Use of judgment and considerateness in dealing with students

6. Rapport with students
7. Self-control and poise
8. Stimulates motivation and enthusiasm for subject
9. Shows creativity, imagination, resourcefulness

Comments: _____

_____

_____

_____

_____

Other Comments and Summary: _____

_____

_____

_____

_____

_____

_____

_____

_____

Recommendations: _____

_____

_____

_____

_____

_____

_____

_____

_____

_____

_____

Date of conference held to discuss
this report:

_____   _____

                                                                    Signature of Evaluator

_____   _____

                                                                    Signature of Teacher*

*In signing this form the teacher does not necessarily indicate agreement with its contents. The signature indicates only that the teacher has read the form. Teachers may if they wish add their own comments on a separate sheet of paper, which will be attached to this observation report.

FIGURE 4-4

Public School
Observation Report

Date: _____

School: _____   Size of Class Observed: _____

Teacher: _____   Length of Observation: _____

Grade or Subject: _____   Level of Class Observed: _____

OBSERVATION: may comment on any of the "criteria for effective teaching" observed.

Over

_____
OBSERVER

COPY TO:
      TEACHER
      PRINCIPAL
      OTHER _____

Balance of Claims, Evidence, Interpretations and Judgments

So far we have made the case that only narrative reports on blank paper allow a skillful observer to comment on all the significant instructional events he/she observes, free of the restrictions of limiting categories. Second, we have argued that only narrative reports allow observers to comment at appropriate length on significant events and to show the flow of teaching-learning episodes and their relation to one another. Now, we will argue that only narrative reports allow observers to write with a balance of *claims, evidence, interpretations* and *judgments,* elements which are essential to effective feedback to teachers about their teaching.

All four of these elements must be present in appropriate proportions for writing (or speaking) about observed teaching to communicate effectively.

> A *claim* is a generalization about a person's teaching. For example, "He is very alert to management problems that could block class momentum."

> *Evidence* is a literal description of something the observer heard or saw to back up the claim. "Walking past Stephen, he passed him a pencil without pausing and continued the discussion of double jeopardy."

> *Interpretations* explain why the evidence does, indeed, support the claim. Interpretations typically start with "thus" and "therefore" statements; they contain an inferred, "as a result of this behavior, what the teacher accomplished was…and here's why." To put it another way, interpretations tell what the teacher or the incident accomplished or intended to accomplish. For example, "thus he got Stephen started with notetaking without skipping a beat in the discussion." All pieces of evidence do not require interpretations in write-ups, but some really do.

> *Judgments* let the reader know what the observer thought of the observed event. "This was an excellent way to re-engage Stephen." Sometimes judgments are built into the syntax of a claim and a separate judgmental sentence is unnecessary as in the claim sentence above.

Stringing claims, evidence, interpretations and judgments together in almost any order, we get effective paragraphs. Figure 4-5 summarizes these definitions and gives additional examples of each; it also gives examples of how they can easily be assembled into paragraphs.

FIGURE 4-5

Analysis: Translating it into Writing

Claim: a statement that a teacher performs a certain teaching skill or carries out a certain pattern in his/her instruction (thus, a *generalization*.)

"He makes a point of coming back to students who are confused."

"He is alert to management problems that could block class momentum."

Evidence: a *quote or literal description* of something said or done.

He said, "I don't want to drop you just yet, Maria. What would be the next step?"

"Walking past Stephen, he passed him a pencil without pausing and continued the discussion of double jeopardy."

Interpretation: a statement of *what the behavior accomplished* or intended to accomplish or what was significant about it.

"With this question he made sure she understood the steps that had come before.

"Thus he got Stephen started with note-taking without skipping a beat."

Judgment: a sentence, phrase or adjective that lets the reader know what the writer thought of the behavior.

"He is effective at coming back to students who are confused."

"He either avoids them or handles them so smoothly one hardly notices them."

Putting all four elements together one might see the following:

He is effective at coming back to students who are confused to make sure they understand key points. "I don't want to drop you just yet, Maria. What would be the next step?" With this question he made sure she understood the steps that had come before.

OR

Next he said, "I don't want to stop you just yet, Maria. What would be the next step?" In this way he showed his thoroughness in making sure students understand. Not only did he return to Maria, he checked with a question she could answer only if she understood the 3 steps Matt had given.

He is alert to management problems. He either avoids them or handles them so smoothly that one hardly notices them. Walking past Stephen, he passed him a pencil without pausing and continued the discussion of double jeopardy. Thus he got Stephen started note-taking without skipping a beat.

OR

He knows what's going on all over the room and makes unobtrusive management moves so things keep moving along. For example, when he noticed Stephen had no pencil and was not taking notes, he walked past him and casually passed him a pencil from behind his ear, all the while continuing the discussion of double jeopardy without missing a beat. Stephen started taking notes.

Writing in this way provides the specifics and the structure to be convincing in evaluation, whether we are trying to praise and recognize outstanding performance or call attention to problems. Figure 4-6 contrasts the effectiveness of write-ups that do and do not have specific evidence to back up claims.

In addition to claims, evidence, interpretations and judgments, many observation write-ups can contain appropriate suggestions[1]. Suggestions do not necessarily imply the teacher committed errors and need not be synonymous with "remediation." Good supervisors often stretch the thinking of good teachers by suggesting one consider alternate or additional strategies simply for the sake of broadening a teacher's repertoire. "Before you start your next novel, it might be interesting to ask the students what they know, think they know and want to know after you've shown them the title, author and picture on the cover." This suggestion is made not because the teacher had a clumsy introduction, but simply to offer an idea the teacher might like to try.

On the other hand, when lessons go poorly and observers produce critical write-ups, it is incumbent on them also to offer suggestions on how to improve in as concrete and specific ways as possible. (See write-up of Kathleen Sutton in Appendix B.)

Literal Notes

Figure 4-6 summarizes the case for taking literal notes during classroom observations. The point is that no matter what the purpose of the observation and conference and no matter what the level of development of the teacher, there are advantages to having plentiful, accurate, literal notes of what transpired. By literal we mean either quotes from teachers and students or objective descriptions of actions ("walks down side aisle...touches George's shoulder.")

Good notes:

- consist of quotes and descriptions of behavior or space and materials,

- capture the essence of important events, actions, conversations, occasionally noting what time it is,

- include specific names,

- record factual observations, not analysis or inferences, and

- describe characteristics of interactions or settings.

---

[1] If a class is superb, however, the evaluator should not feel *obliged* to come up with a suggestion just because it is a norm in the district for evaluators to give suggestions.

Effects of Having/Not Having Literal Data

We give teachers feedback from observations for at least four different purposes. What is the effect of having concrete and literal information for them in each of these situations?

Don't have
literal data

Do have
literal data

Situation 1: Cheerleading — for people doing a great job.

They know I'm supportive. They know I like them...or they know they got through this evaluation OK...but they may still feel vulnerable in front of other observers who may not "like" their teaching.

They know *what* they are doing effectively and *how*.
...leads to feeling strong and competent within oneself.
internal orientation which helps people grow strong.

Situation 2: Enrichment —for people looking for something new...(or in a rut and you want to help them get reinvigorated)... both the self-motivated, reflective person and the stagnant.

They tend to brush off the feedback or the write-ups which don't mean much to them one way or the other.

They may be taken or intrigued by an idea to try something in a new way. You are a resource for ideas for them...or you may be acting as an effective mirror, enabling them to see things about themselves and stimulate them to ask important questions of their own teaching.

Situation 3: Improvement — for people secure in their jobs but who have some teaching issues worth improving.

They don't really know what you *mean*. They feel the criticism but don't really accept it...or they'd like to change and improve but they really don't know what to do.

They see what you mean and see some things to try.

Situation 4: Real Problems — for people who are doing a bad job or who don't belong with children or people for whom there is a *significant* difference in quality

The teacher has no chance of improving because they don't really see or accept what's being said is wrong.

There is a possibility for improvement if there is real willingness from both supervisor and teacher to work on it.

defensive

perhaps willing
to consider
other careers

your case *will* stand up
in court

perhaps unwilling
to consider
alternative careers

your case probably
won't stand up in
court

It is important not to record feelings, judgments, or conclusions during the actual observation; these reactions one will remember afterwards anyway, but exactly what was said or done to make one feel that way will not. Therefore it is essential to concentrate on recording literal data during the in-class visit and save the analysis and inference making until later.

Developing skills at taking this kind of notes takes time and formal practice and is best done with one's colleagues in group settings. Simultaneously training should focus on analyzing the notes for claims and possible interpretations of observed teaching events. Finally, this development of note-taking skills should address strategies for getting efficient at recording what's important and not losing visual contact with the teacher and students.

Final Evaluation Write-Up

Our discussion of writing so far has focused on classroom observation write-ups. But there is another important document to consider—the Final Evaluation Summary document at the end of the year which pulls together the main points of the observations and goes beyond them to comment on the teacher's performance in other roles.

A good evaluation system should allow evaluators—more, should require them by the categories of its paper form— to comment on a teacher's performance in other roles besides interactive classroom teaching. All teachers perform in five important roles about which we can and should give them feedback. They act as:

1. Classroom teachers,

2. Contributing members of the staff,

3. Communicators with parents and community,

4. Performers of routine administrative duties and obligations, and

5. Constant learners responsible for their own professional development.

"Contributing member of the staff" leads us to look at such behaviors as how teachers function at department meetings; how they interact with peers on curriculum committees and other task forces; how they reach out to new teachers. In many ways, teachers do things to help colleagues, build team spirit and further the collaborative goals of the school. This section of the evaluation report is where an evaluator summarizes feedback on how well the teacher works with other professionals. Including this role in teacher evaluation signals that we expect teachers to play a positive role in the organization outside their classrooms.

How well teachers communicate with parents and the broader community is another important role of the job. One can observe such performance at Back-to-School night, during parent conferences and at the numerous points of contact between teachers and parent and community members. This section of an evaluation write-up is the place to note any projects or ways in which a teacher has made an effort to give information to parents or build bridges between the school and the community. It is also the place to note any obstacles the teacher may be posing to good communication.

Teachers are also expected to perform routine administrative functions such as hall duty, cafeteria duty, taking attendance and filling out reports and ordering new materials. It is legitimate to comment on how well they carry out these responsibilities.

The fifth section for comment, "Own professional development," signals that we expect teachers to be constant learners and we want to credit them for the efforts they make toward their own professional growth. By the same token, we need to be able to use evaluation to deal with a teacher who gets in a rut and will do nothing to stretch and learn. Examples of faculty evaluation handbooks incorporating all these roles can be found in Appendices C and D.

Final evaluation forms, like observation forms, should be blank paper, allowing the evaluator to say what needs saying. Similar to narrative observation reports, the final evaluation report should have a heading which says: "This report will comment on the teacher's performance in each the following five roles:" …and then list the five roles. The writer of the report decides where to start and stop each section and marks it with a Roman numeral I-V. How long each section actually turns out to be will depend on how much data the evaluator has to report. Obviously, the section on classroom teaching will and should be far longer than most of the others—in most cases about five times longer. But if good observation reports have been done, the "Classroom Teacher" part of the annual final evaluation summary document need only summarize the major claims from the observations. It does not need to repeat all the evidence or recount all the events from those classes. The purpose now is to summarize those observation reports in about a page of text.

The other four sections may, in fact, contain only a few sentences each. The exception would be, for example, the case of a teacher who has done something significant with community members that helped the school. Thus, for this person, Section IV of the report would be longer than a few sentences. Another example would be a teacher who has terrible relations with other staff members to the degree that it is impeding the successful functioning of the staff. In this case, Section II of the report would be longer and contain claims and evidence just like we expect classroom observation reports to contain. An example of a final evaluation report following these principals can be found in Appendix E.

Rating and Ranking Teachers

In contrast to the narrative final evaluations just described, rating a teacher's behavior on a scale is, at best, uninformative, and ultimately accomplishes little. Ratings focus teachers more on scores than on substance. Like anyone rated on anything, teachers want to know their bottom line "score" right away: how many unsatisfactories, how many satisfactories, how many excellents? Then they want to know how others scored and where they stand in the ranks. ("Did everyone score low? It must be the evaluator." "Did everyone score high and I didn't? You must not have observed carefully." "Did I score high and others low? Whew, glad I got through that one.")

The more points there are in the rating scale, the harder it is to justify numerical distinctions. Teachers with less than the top rating on an item usually want to know what they have to do to get there. "What is the difference between a 4 and a 5 on classroom management? Marcia got a 5. What do I have to do?" And often, administrators are not able to tell them.

Above all, the reason for not using rating scales is that they become a force pressing to restrict the free exchange of ideas among teachers. These are anti-collegial and anti-experimentation, as well. They incline people to play it safe and not risk a lesson that bombs. It puts teachers in competition with one another for...what? For points! —just like we do in some of our more negatively competitive classrooms for children.

Ratings and Merit Pay vs Career Ladders

In this section we'd like to contrast merit pay with career ladders and consider both in relation to rating scales for teacher performance.

Merit pay systems have been instituted and then phased out in dozens of scattered locations throughout the country over the last several decades. These pay schemes have usually met a quick demise, the exceptions being districts where they have remained low-key, optional for teachers and small in scale (Cohen & Murnane, 1985.)

Whenever merit pay has been initiated, the evaluation instruments have inevitably created multiple rating scales so as to quantify judgments about who gets merit pay and who doesn't. We would argue, however, that raw merit pay does not justify rating teachers and rating of teachers cannot and should not support merit pay distinctions between teachers.

Gabor (1990) cites Edward Deming, the distinguished management consultant known as the "man who brought the quality revolution to America", who asserts:

> A merit rating is alluring. The sound of the words captivates the imagination: pay for what you get; get what you pay for; motivate people to do their best, for their own good. The effect is exactly the opposite of what those words promise. Everyone propels himself forward, or tries to, for his own good, on his own life preserver. The organization is the loser. The merit rating rewards people [who] conform to the system. It does not reward attempts to improve the system. (p. 251.)

Merit pay attempts to motivate improved performance and reward it with money. It is "baloney," as Phil Schlecty (1986) says, to think that merit pay will motivate performance and improve teaching. Numerous studies of teachers (see Devaney, 1987) tell us that their primary motivators are a sense of efficacy with students and the satisfactions of professional growth that come from collaboration with colleagues. Merit pay also can be pernicious. It diverts teachers from substance, focuses them on PR with their evaluators and puts them in competition with one another.

> The idea of trying to differentiate on some fine-grained system is ridiculous. You can't make those kinds of discriminations on total performance. Total performance is a complex collage of competency, skills and knowledge. Most people are in the middle, and what we need to do is identify the really outstanding performers and the really poor performers and try not to pretend that one can make [fine-line] differentiations objectively. (Michael Beer, Harvard Business School in Gabor, op. cit., pp. 251-52.)

And citing Deming again:

> The merit rating nourishes short term performance, annihilates long-term planning, builds fear, demolishes teamwork, nourishes rivalry and politics. It leaves people bitter, crushed, bruised, battered, desolate, despondent, dejected, feeling inferior, some even depressed, unfit for work for weeks after receipt of rating, unable to comprehend why they are inferior. It is unfair as it ascribes to the people in a group differences that may be caused totally by the system they work in. (Gabor, op. cit, p. 253)

Deming believes that

> ...most people want, and deserve, to take joy in their work. It is management's moral obligation to create a system that enables them to do so. Given a chance by management and the system, most people will seek fulfillment in their work by doing the best they can. (Gabor, op. cit., p. 253.)

A career ladder, on the other hand, as distinct from merit pay, could reward superior service and skill with promotion and the opportunity to assume leadership in important and interesting areas of school life. Top rung on a ladder would be a gateway into such positions. A genuine career ladder could be a giant step in the professionalization of teaching; and teacher evaluation could play a legitimate role in identifying teachers whose performance has earned them the right to additional career opportunities. While teacher salaries in general must be made more competitive, pay-for-performance does not have the motivating effect that enhanced job opportunities would have.

When new roles are created for teachers, it may require evaluation systems that certify a certain standard of teaching competence for those who would apply for these new positions. But it is more likely that differentiated positions within teaching would be filled by matching an applicant's proficiencies with the specific job requirements of the new position rather than filling these positions by some measured metric of teaching skill. For example, as many excellent baseball players would not make good coaches or managers, it takes more than personal teaching skill to be a good mentor or to be an organizer of a mentor program.

Rewarding teachers with bonuses for good performance may have a place in schools; but if it does, it will be in rewarding *teams* of teachers or whole *buildings* for achieving worthwhile goals for children.

Teacher Goal Setting

Many districts include a teacher goal-setting component in their evaluation process. This is highly desirable as long as it isn't the *whole* evaluation process. A teacher goal-setting process recognizes that teachers are professionals who have insight into what their students need and what they themselves need for professional improvement. It is appropriate then that a teacher's evaluation includes a significant place for evaluating progress toward something the teacher personally owns and thinks is important. Just *having* such a process impels teachers to do self-evaluation (or needs assessments for their classes) and to pick worthwhile improvement goals. Such a process is respectful of teachers and stimulates professional improvement.

Guidelines for making teacher goal-setting effective include:

1. Have few goals—1, 2, or 3 serious, substantive ones at most. Targeting too many goals fragments one's efforts and leads to frustration or the trivializing of the goals.

2. Make sure one of the goals pertains to instruction. That is the heart of our business.

3. Develop in-service training for teachers on how to set realistic, attainable goals and how to use the well-refined knowledge that exists about making good plans of action to realize goals.

4. Goals from last year may be continued into this year. There is no need to come up with a totally new set of goals each year. In fact, some of the most worthwhile goals (e.g., learning how to use cooperative learning techniques to raise achievement and cultivate respect for human differences) take several years to achieve. Thus evaluators should not negatively judge partial fulfillment of significant, self-set goals of teachers when real effort has been expended and real progress can be reported.

5. There is a place for evaluators to set goals for teachers, but it is a small one. When a person's teaching is seriously deficient, the evaluator should be entitled to set goals for that teacher which are specific and helpful. When that happens, however, we have moved away from the main purpose of teacher goal-setting, which is to stimulate self-analysis and self-development.

6. It is legitimate for each teacher to include a system-wide goal in their personal goals and to be accountable through evaluation for progress toward such a goal.

Earlier in this monograph we proposed that one of the things it takes to make supervision and evaluation really work is that leadership sees to it that the system's *"structures, resources and cultural expectations support teachers and administrators viewing themselves as constant learners."* The goal-setting procedures we have just described provide such a structure. But the structure by itself will not communicate the *cultural expectation* that all adults in the school be constant learners; it merely provides an open channel for that communication. The communication of the message will come through the words and the attitudes of the evaluator in face-to-face contact with the teacher.

If you are my evaluator and you want to convey an expectation for constant adult learning, then your words, your modeling and your body language will tell me that you believe "no one knows it all"; that I am not flawed as a teacher or a human being for having doubts, questions and problems I'm working on with my class; and that when I participate in evaluation, *you expect me* to identify frontiers for my own growth and what I'm doing about them. Thus I will understand that your writing in my final evaluation document each year about "areas of growth" as a teacher (and your information on what I'm doing may, in fact, come from me) is not a criticism of me but a symbol and a reminder of one facet of our view of professionals: constant learners. Through this goal setting process, administrators set the climate described above.

Self-Evaluation of Teachers

It is also very productive to ask teachers to write a self-evaluation at some point in their cycle of professional growth. Administrators who do so ask for a written set of goal statements at the beginning of the year and a narrative in the spring from the teacher describing what was done and what progress was achieved. When administrators take these seriously, they signal that they do so by reading the self-evaluations carefully and having conferences with all teachers in turn about the written analyses.

These conferences are a wonderful opportunity to communicate interest and support for teachers' self-set goals. The process itself communicates trust in the teacher's judgment to pick a worthwhile goal for his/her own development. It further communicates trust in the teacher's ability to work seriously and report honestly on his/her progress. In these conferences, administrators who are school culture builders use their active-listening skills and put themselves in a position to be a facilitator of a teacher's thinking.

Administrators also put themselves into the information flow. By reading written self-evaluations, administrators get a tremendous amount of information they would not otherwise come across (nor would anyone else) about what teachers are doing in their classrooms.

Finally, and perhaps most significantly, by causing teachers to *write* about what they are doing, self-evaluations actually stimulate and advance teachers' *thinking* about what they do. As Henry Glassie (1982) says, "I write what I know to find out what I think."

Teacher Evaluation of Administrators

For administrators to solicit systematic feedback from teachers about their own performance is rare. Yet to do so is a fine model for the kind of open communication and trust we want to be developing in the culture of the school. In addition to giving otherwise unobtainable and very useful feedback to administrators (for it is rare for a teacher to march in and address the boss's strengths and weaknesses), such a practice would enable the administrator to model using feedback to alter practice. That is, after all, only a normal and sensible way to proceed. One would expect it to be the accepted norm in any group of adults. Yet we find many schools where the culture of "perfection on paper" prevails, that is, teachers find a written suggestion to try something different intolerable. It is, somehow, unacceptable to be anything less than perfect (at least in one's image on paper). If the leader/administrator solicits written suggestions and is willing to acknowledge their value, then we are much less likely to see teachers react with paranoia to written suggestions.

Can Evaluators Supervise?

There are those who say supervision must be separated from evaluation because it is impossible for teachers to open up and have productive, growth-oriented dialog with one who judges them. In other words, teacher evaluation is incompatible with stimulating teachers' thinking and growth. We reject that notion. The problem is not that evaluators can't supervise, it is that they cannot supervise often enough.

Some of you (regrettably not many) reading this piece know that evaluation can be good supervision because you have had principals or department chairs who evaluated you and simultaneously stretched your thinking, challenged your ideas about practice, respected you as a decision-maker and helped you grow as a teacher. There is no inherent reason why an evaluator cannot build trust with a teacher and have meaningful two-way dialog about observed teaching. We would agree that it doesn't *happen* all that often, but there is no positional or psychological reason this must be. All we need is for evaluators to behave in certain ways:

1. come in and observe frequently enough,
2. speak directly and honestly to teachers,
3. produce feedback that is helpful and informed by knowledge about teaching and about good observing, and
4. see their mission primarily as stimulating and advancing teachers' thinking about their instructional decisions (thus willing to give data and raise questions without rushing to judgment).

The point is often made that the success of feedback between observer and observee depends on a trusting relationship. While that is true, it omits the point that the road to trust goes through the land of quality. Quality in the feedback is the key. If I know my job is secure, then what is most important about the feedback I get is that it be *quality*. If I get useful feedback from you, I will come to trust both you and the process (Natriello, 1984 and Duke & Stiggins, 1990).

Unfortunately, in most schools in America the gap between the four conditions above and the reality of teachers' experience of evaluation is immense. Teacher evaluation has been a joke in American education, either non-existent or a sham, until as recently as ten years ago. But that situation has been changing rapidly. To change it requires:

  a. a district-wide commitment to doing evaluation well;

  b. administrators well-trained in observing and analyzing teaching (which we have the technology to do now); and

  c. professionals who have sufficient time and access to work with teachers on examining their teaching.

This third requirement is by far the hardest to achieve and most revolutionary in scope.

If a principal supervises eight to twelve people (the commonly agreed maximum span of control in business and industry) the principal can give these people frequent, high-quality observational feedback. It will not matter that the person also passes judgment on their performance. Gary Natriello's research has already established that even in public schools, good feedback that is frequent enough makes converts of teachers who started out as fierce resisters to evaluation. That it's *called* evaluation ceases to matter if people find the feedback productive.

To get this frequency and quality of feedback, regardless of who does it (evaluator, staff developer, department chair, peer observer) or what it's called (supervision, evaluation, peer review, collegial coaching), will require a public investment in training and in redefined job descriptions that will raise the cost of schooling. Since, however, it will undoubtedly raise the *quality* of schooling, it's one of the best investments imaginable at a time when the reform movement is looking for key points at which to intervene. In the next chapter we will describe what has been done by school districts committed to raising the frequency and quality of feedback to teachers with current resources and organizational structures.

A final note regarding "evaluators'" ability to engage in growth-oriented dialog with teachers they observe: what if your job is not secure, and the first instance of quality feedback you get from me is negative? How can you trust me and open up to a productive dialog with me?

If you're a non-tenured teacher, you will, indeed, experience anxiety if the feedback is negative. There is no avoiding that, so evaluators shouldn't lose any sleep over it. In the case of a struggling non-tenured teacher, I cannot let my desire to keep their anxiety low interfere with my honesty. Confronting the issues with the teacher and then being as helpful as possible (including hooking the teacher up with colleagues) is the fairest and most growth-stimulating thing I can do for that teacher. What I *can* do regarding their anxiety, if I am in an evaluative role with a non-tenured teacher, is to tell them as early as possible whether or not I see their current level of performance as acceptable (translation: contract renewable)—especially if I am delivering some negative feedback. I owe them that—and I greatly increase the chances that the teacher and I can focus on the substance of the teaching issues. Trust grows out of quality interactions.

Now let us turn to "frequent, high quality feedback" and see what can be done to make it happen. In the first chapter of this monograph we said that overall:

1. We want our system for observing teachers to give adults *frequent, quality feedback* on their practice from *someone who knows what they are talking about.* (Cheerleading, Facilitating, Stimulating, Problem Solving)

2. We want our system for observing teachers to produce judgments about the performance level and job status of teachers, and most importantly, whether they are or are not performing up to district standards. (Monitoring, Directing, Assigning, Remediating and Dismissing)

We have spent most of our time until now describing principles, procedures and forms for taking care of the second cluster above. In the previous section ("Can Evaluators Supervise?") we claimed evaluators could deliver frequent, high quality feedback to teachers if they were skilled, if their span of control were small enough (eight to twelve) and if there were no structural obstacles in their way (like merit pay.) But their span of control is not small enough, nor will it be in the foreseeable future. Thus how then can we arrange for true "supervision" for teachers given our current resources?

V.
Making
Supervision Work

Arranging for frequent,
high-quality
feedback to teachers

MAKING SUPERVISION WORK

This chapter is about creating frequent high quality observational feedback for teachers, which has been our working definition of "supervision" since Chapter I. Before looking at the specifics of how to accomplish this goal, it is important to place it in a larger context.

Overall, what we want is a *professional culture of reflection, feedback and discourse about teaching practice* among a faculty. Elsewhere (Saphier and King, 1985) we have written about the constellation of behavior patterns among adults that generates and nourishes an environment where this professional culture can thrive. And we know that when we get such an environment, we get better learning for children. A line of studies starting with Rutter in 1979 and followed by a steady succession of others (see Appendix H) has confirmed the importance of a strong school culture among adults if we want good schools for children. Institutionalizing frequent, high quality observational feedback to teachers is only one element of such a strong culture, but it is a particularly potent and important one. In subsequent sections of this chapter, as we address how to make practical arrangements for these frequent observations, please remember that we are doing so from within a broader set of goals, goals having to do with strengthening school culture on twelve particular norms of behavior.

- Collegiality
- Experimentation
- Reaching Out to the Knowledge Base
- High Expectations
- Caring, Celebration and Humor
- Traditions
- Tangible Support
- Protecting What's Important
- Appreciation and Recognition
- Respect and Confidence
- Involvement in Decision-Making
- Honest, Open Communication

Schools that get results for children are schools where adult staff members feel good, work hard, keep learning and believe that together they can make a difference for kids. At one level this is only common sense, but in the priorities and practice of American schools it is an uncommon focus.

Suprisingly it is only in the last decade that researchers have investigated the link between the quality of life in the workplace for adults and the productivity of the school for children. It is not surprising, however, that we now have good data to back up the claim above (Rutter 1979, Little 1982, Purkey and Smith 1983, Rosenholtz 1989).

The argument is deceivingly simple, but its components are many and subtle. The argument is this: the foundation of progress, the foundation of a plan—any plan—for school improvement is the energy and productive working relationships of the people in the organization. If the school as a workplace is challenging, satisfying and growth-oriented for adults, it liberates the creativity and energy of those who shape it...no matter how good it is now, they constantly work to make it better.

Not only do we now know this to be true, we know a good deal about the elements of such an energized, productive environment. They include the twelve elements listed above, and strengthening them must be the overarching commitment of any school organization that wants to get real and enduring results for children. There is, indeed, a connection between the strength of these norms and the ease with which one will be able to implement the suggestions in the balance of this chapter. Creating a culture of frequent observation is a revolutionary culture shift.

Henry Brickell (1984) frequently asks large audiences of educators to think of the jobs they have held outside education. He then asks individuals to tell how often they were observed in their role by someone who is in a position to give them feedback on performance and did so. He gets comments from people who have been everything from servers at McDonald's to project managers in high tech companies. Typical answers are: "weekly," "every few days," "daily," "biweekly." When he asks the same questions about people's teaching, Brickell gets "every three years," "once, in 1976," "once or twice a year," "15 years ago," and a couple of "nevers."

This dearth of feedback is an appalling reality in teaching and one that drastically reduces the rate of teachers' own learning and improvement. A potent step we could take to improve both teachers' teaching and their job satisfaction would be to dramatically increase teachers' contact with each other for purposes of dialog and for structured, specific feedback. But in the culture of today's schools, that is a very difficult issue to broach for reasons that have been explored elsewhere (Lieberman and Miller, 1979; Lieberman, 1988). These include:

- the conception of teaching exclusively as an art,

- the belief that the knowledge base of the craft is weak[1]

---

[1] ...which we strongly dispute. Part of the argument of this monograph is that we not only *have* a knowledge about the craft, but that to have good evaluation we must systematically build in training for administrators in the observation and analysis of teaching through the lenses of this knowledge base.

- the structural isolation of teachers from one another through the design of physical space and time schedules, and

- the lack of appreciation and of confidence teachers experience about the quality of their work, which no one sees but their students.

Our long drought from feedback has so accustomed us to isolation that efforts to make teaching more open to public view are sometimes greeted with indignant posturings about professional privilege on the one hand and paranoia about being judged on the other. Zahorik (1987) in a poignant article about teachers' sources of support, chronicles how difficult it was for best friends, teaching in the same grade in adjacent rooms for many years, to break through habits of privacy and give each other observational feedback. Yet we know with some certainty that exchanging ideas and getting feedback from other professionals is a peak experience for teachers, rare as it may be (Devaney, 1987). We also know that it is an essential ingredient in effective schools (Little, 1982). Thus we must exert our best efforts to increase the amount of observational feedback teachers receive.

In the sections that follow we will examine 1) how to create conditions in which peer observations not only thrive, but become part of the culture of a school; 2) how to use multiple year evaluation cycles to institutionalize peer observation; and 3) how the scheduling and grouping structures of schools can encourage more public teaching by teachers in front of one another.

Making Peer Observations Work

Just how valuable are focused observations when conducted by peers who are non-evaluative personnel? They are not only independently valuable in terms of being productive for teaching and learning, but also *inherently satisfying* for the teachers who take part. They feel good. Never having done them, however, most teachers are anxious about the notion of peer observations and reluctant to try one. This was the case in a district where we recently completed an in-service course for 40 teachers, K-12.

The course required a peer-observation with a report to us of 1) what "experiment" teachers had tried, 2) what feedback they had gotten from their colleague, 3) what they had altered or modified as a result of the feedback, and 4) what they had learned from the experience. Their comments were universally positive (including people who had been resistant in the sessions and critical of parts of the course.) It was common to find statements such as:

"Walls came tumbling down between teachers..."

"It was wonderful to have a chance to really talk to someone about what I was trying..."

"Conversations spilled over into the teachers room and involved us with each other in a way we never had before..."

"This was the best part of the course."

"With the feedback and our discussion I was able to solve a problem that had been bothering me a long time..."

"Just preparing for the pre-conference helped me think through the problem and what I wanted to do."

These are not uncommon reactions to well-structured peer observations. Does it not seem unusual, then, that they are so rare. In my experience, peer observation takes place for only about one out of every hundred teachers, once a year.

Peer observations are an optimal way to generate the sense of collegiality and experimentation so missing in the life of teachers (Little, 1982). Yet efforts at peer observation have an erratic history similar in baseball to the quest for pitching the perfect game—much desired, often tried, seldom sustained. As a result peer observation is not taken seriously today and thrives more in print than in action. This is unwarranted and unnecessary.

For peer observations to work (which means for them to energize teachers and, indeed, the whole school culture), five things are needed:

- *time,*

- an *attitude of experimentation,*

- a specific *focus,*

- *training in giving feedback,* and

- clear *expectations.*

Time

Here's a $1,000 idea.[1] Hire a sub one day a week for the building. The sub is only allowed to substitute for teachers who are visiting each other, not for sick people. The sub brings his or her own enrichment lesson so the teacher doesn't have to spend extra hours preparing plans for the sub and mopping up afterwards.

Hire the person in advance and line them up for a regular day each week for the whole year (or perhaps for 20 weeks excluding the beginning and ending months of school). Get a really good person, perhaps a recently retired teacher or a teacher on maternity leave, pay her above the standard rate and ask her to prepare an inventory of lessons for the grade range of your school. She is expected to bring these lessons with her, ready to go. Three or four lessons per grade will suffice, meaning only 18-24 prepared lessons for a K-5 school, half that for a middle school, junior high or high school. (Furthermore, that gives enough coverage for every teacher to do three or four peer observations a year.)

The lessons are enrichment lessons—say around critical thinking—which will run with any class. These subs are a real gift for teachers; they don't create more work than they're worth, offer something of value to kids and give professional teachers real time—otherwise unavailable—to do peer observations.

Time has been a big obstacle in the past. Suppose two teachers, Jane and Fred, are both teaching a new curriculum. They want to observe each other and talk afterwards to give feedback and trade ideas. Most often, however, Jane's preparation period does not coincide with the block when Fred teaches the new unit. So Jane has to make all kinds of arrangements and ask for favors to get her class covered for 50 minutes so she can visit Fred. Maybe she'll do it once if she's really motivated, but not often. And without some special incentive she may never do it at all. With the provisions above, these time and coverage problems disappear.

Other ways to gain time are summarized in Joyce and Showers (1988). For example, there are frequently periods when one teacher could productively teach a large group lesson where presentation and demonstration are appropriate to two parallel classes (i.e., two fourth grades or two sections of sophomore biology), thus freeing one teacher for an observation.

Attitude

If observations are to become a regular part of school life, it is important that teachers see the payoff they can get from them. Staff members must be very clear that these visits are aimed at increasing both the quality and the frequency of adult contact in the workplace. Observations can provide the vehicle for improving their

---

[1] We get $1,000 by taking $45 per day and boosting it to $50 to give something extra to a person who is expected to come with prepared lessons. $50 x 20 weeks = $1,000.

teaching and for solving classroom problems. They must also realize that the activity is safe. For these attitudes to prevail, there need to be some common agreements about why we are setting up the observations. We have used a handout with teachers to establish such a common ground that includes the following content:

The purpose of the peer observation/visitation is to provide an opportunity to strengthen collegiality and experimentation as norms of our professional climate.

Each of you is asked to pick something you'd like to try (or have been trying) out of the knowledge bases we've been exploring. You tell a colleague from this course what you're experimenting with and ask him/her to observe and give you feedback on what you're doing. The feedback could be around how much of a new behavior you're doing (say, how much "wait-time" if you're trying that one); feedback could be around how accurately you're following the steps of some new model of teaching; or it could be around appropriateness as you mutually discuss when and with whom you're using the strategy. What you try and what kind of feedback you solicit are up to you and your observer to determine. The point of the exercise is to leave you the flexibility to experiment with something you find interesting and significant and to make the observation helpful to you in developing your skill. It is also an opportunity for your colleague to serve as an observer and practice his/her note-taking, listening and reflective questioning skills.

The nice thing about "experimentation" as an idea is it allows you to be not proficient at something. After all, we're trying something new, and rarely does one do something new without making mistakes or finding bugs. It is professionally rewarding to have both the help and the companionship of a colleague as one goes through such experiments. That is what this visitation is all about.

When experimentation is a cultural norm in a school, people are encouraged and rewarded for experimenting, even if the experiment doesn't work. They are encouraged to reach for new and interesting ideas and give them a fair trial, discarding what seems inappropriate and incorporating what works. When collegiality is a norm, teachers are not isolated, there is much practical talk about teaching and people are constantly helping and learning from one another. This exercise thus seeks to create an event for each of you— an event that might not otherwise happen in the busy press of the school year— for you to experience an added dimension of experimentation and collegiality with one another.

The main thing is to go for it—stretch to try something new and give yourself the gift of a colleague's companionship as you do so (as well as giving that gift in return).

Something like the above must be agreed upon so the staff shares these understandings: our purposes are experimentation, helping each other and stretching for new learning. As explicitly as possible, we work to build trust by accepting as our charter the following:

1. I believe in your positive motivations. (I believe your intentions with kids are the best.)

2. I respect your position as the ultimate decision-maker (about what you're doing with kids).

3. We're doing this work together to help each other grow…expand our repertoires…stimulate each others' thinking…(acknowledges everybody has room to grow and learn).

4. We have something to learn from every other person.

5. I trust that if you see something that you're uncomfortable about or don't understand, you'll tell me…and you will do it from the standpoint of genuine questioning rather than judgment.

There is value in explicitly stating these attitudes as mutual commitments at the beginning of an observation cycle.

Focus
The optimal grounding for a peer observation is this: one is giving colleagues non-evaluative feedback on a *specific experiment* they are trying, not open-ended feedback or a general evaluation of the lesson.

For peer observations to succeed, the observer needs a specific focus. Open-ended observations leave both parties unsure of the purpose of the feedback. The quality of the post-conferences will vary, depending on the ability of the observers to bring some useful lenses of their own to the observation. Sometimes these open-ended observations make the visitors feel they should look for and give positive strokes only; such feedback may leave the observee feeling good, but with little of use to build on.

Conversely, open-ended observations can feel like evaluations, where the observer tells the observee what was good and what wasn't. No matter how skillful one is at giving positive and negative feedback, creating a situation where open-ended evaluation of another person's teaching is expected defeats the collegial purpose. The purpose is to cultivate collegiality, experimentation and reflective thinking, not to evaluate one's general worth as a teacher or even the general success of a given lesson. It is important, therefore, that the peer observer give data and ask reflective questions when giving feedback rather than make judgments. Training and practice in these skills greatly increases the productivity of peer observations (see next section.)

You may have noticed the reference to the "knowledge bases we've been exploring" in the handout quoted above. For their experiments, teachers who received the handout selected strategies presented in an in-service course. The course took up such topics as Clarity, Principles of Learning, Models of Teaching and others. For each topic, a variety of strategies from the knowledge base associated with that topic were presented, demonstrated and then practiced by participants in workshops. Thus each participant had a reservoir of ideas from which to select their experiment, and the peer observers had that reservoir in common.

But one does not need to be taking a course with colleagues to come up with a specific focus for observation. A middle school team may come up with a discipline strategy for a particularly resistant child; a group of teachers in a magazine club may find a reading comprehension strategy in an article that a couple of people would like to try; after a system-wide in-service session, two teachers may decide to try a strategy the speaker mentioned. *Anything* may serve as the source of the idea, as long as experimenting with it and giving collegial support through specific feedback is the purpose of the observation.[1]

Training in Observation and Giving Feedback

The skills of literal note-taking described on earlier in this monograph are as important for teachers giving feedback to each other as for administrators doing evaluation. To stimulate a colleague's thinking about practice in a non-evaluative way one must give data and raise questions. To do that one must *have* data, literal data about what was said and what teachers and students did. Thus work on literal note taking is very helpful for teachers who want peer observations to be productive.

The second form of training that is immensely useful and perhaps necessary is training in how to conduct pre and post conferences, especially how to give data and ask questions in a non-judgmental way. The Cognitive Coaching framework of Costa and Garmston (1990, 1991, 1992) is the best we know of for accomplishing this training. Appendix I contains handouts from our adaptation of this training which provide guidelines for pre and post conferences. We have found that actual training and practice in giving non-judgmental feedback, however, are necessary if these

---

[1] One excellent source of innovative teaching strategies we offer is *Understanding Teaching,* a quarterly newsletter that highlights useful and timely teaching ideas drawn from practitioners, theoreticians and researchers. (Research for Better Teaching, Carlisle, MA)

conferences are to be maximally productive. Thus we have found it beneficial to build such training into our own courses and modules for teachers on the knowledge base on teaching.

Expectations

In our courses, teachers are assigned the task of observing each other. In addition to making the purpose and context as safe as possible, it's easier for them to buy in because they *have* to (it's assigned) and because everyone is in the same boat. But how does one create the expectation that teachers will do regular peer observation when there's no course requirement?

The most important point is that the expectation should be created (and we will take up the means in a minute). Even though the $1,000 substitute idea makes it much easier to do peer observations, and even though it guarantees that the self-starters on one's staff will visit each other, it does not guarantee that the practice will become widespread; it does not guarantee the kind of liberating and energizing effect that is possible school-wide.

So how does one build up the expectation—make it a "behavioral regularity" (Sarason 1982)—that this is what we do, that this is what it means to be a professional in this building, that these peer observations are as much a regular part of the workplace for adults as bus schedules and playground duty? We would propose first, that the expectation must have the formal commitment of the leader—the principal or whomever is the chief administrator; otherwise the resources to secure the practice cannot be counted on (namely, the money, time and effort required to secure a good substitute with a battery of prepared lessons, the management of scheduling and access, etc.). Second, commitment to the practice is probably best generated through some sort of building faculty council or senate. This allows teachers to own as well as sell the practice to their colleagues and allows a gradual spread of the practice throughout the building over a few years rather than muscling everyone into it by mandate.

Expectations can be institutionalized slowly but thoroughly in a school culture through the hiring process. In one district where we work, multiple peer observations *are* mandated, but only for *new teachers* to the district. These observations accompany a required series of in-service sessions about the knowledge base on teaching. The sessions stress collegiality, experimentation and developing one's repertoire of skills, not a 'here's-how-to-do-it" approach. They also provide a built-in support group for new teachers. New teachers are less resistant to required observations because they view them as part of their tenure process. The district views the course and the observations as part of the systematic socialization of new personnel to the values of the school district. And the long-range effect of the whole process is to create a teacher corps (after enough years have gone by) that accepts peer observations as part of its culture.

The purpose of the above example is to describe another way professional exchange might become a regular part of a school's culture—an "expectation." Socializing new teachers to regular peer observations, however, will only have a lasting effect on general practice if building principals and department chairs continue to support and, in fact, explicitly expect it to continue. This expectation could be communicated in many ways, for instance, in beginning-of-the-year speeches, in teachers' goal-setting conferences, through public recognition for teachers who collaborate, or by favoring with resources those who pursue collegiality and experimentation. But communicated it must be. In another district where we have done extensive work on peer observation, all teachers are expected to do several peer observations each year. This expectation applies to veterans and new hires alike.

Teachers feel excitement, empowerment and affiliation when they have time to work together and when that time leads to better ideas and better learning for kids. When two (or more) teachers work together around the substance of their craft, around instructional issues and details of particular lessons, or problems, or skills, those two teachers create synergy, that is, greater productivity than either could have mustered alone. This is true in any field. What is so astonishing is that in teaching, a human services profession, human synergy among practitioners is so difficult to achieve. It is systematically and structurally excluded from the workplace by the institution. Now it is time to systematically and structurally build it *in*.

Multiple Year Evaluation Cycles

We recommend evaluating teachers formally once every four years (with the option, of course, of evaluating any teacher any year if there are serious concerns about performance.) This cycle reduces the load on administrators and enables them to spend extensive, high quality time working with a manageable number of teachers. The question then becomes: what happens for teachers in the intervening years? Are they left purely to their own devices? How can we structure activities that are not evaluative yet are productive for teacher growth in those intervening years and also arrange for good observational feedback not connected with evaluation? The following is a case study of a district that addressed exactly those questions.

Building Collegiality, Experimentation and Reflection into a Professional Growth Cycle—a Case Study

In New York State a district in which we work started its comprehensive planning process for a revised evaluation form by sending the following to all faculty as a joint letter signed by the union president and the superintendent.

Dear Colleagues,

All plans for supervision and evaluation aim at continuous improvement of instruction. We want ours to as well. But in addition we would like to come up with a professional growth plan that achieves more.

The State of New York has required that a written statement of performance be done each year on every teacher. Therefore it is necessary to reexamine what we do in each year of the current four-year evaluation cycle. We would like this re-examination to produce a plan with broad-based support throughout the district and use it as an opportunity to move ahead rather than just meet a state regulation. Move ahead toward what?... toward a professional growth cycle that would achieve the following outcomes:

PROFESSIONAL GROWTH CYCLE

1. *Every year teachers have a chance for substantive, helpful conversations about their teaching with someone who is knowledgeable about what they do and can help them reflect on their decision-making with students. (Teaching is too isolated and lonely a profession.)*

2. *The school as a workplace becomes a more satisfying, growth-oriented environment for adults. (The better the working environment for adults, the better the learning for students.) Thus the plan must manifest our commitment to the development of people at all stages in their careers.*

3. *The district has a clear and fair set of procedures for dealing with teachers whose performance is less than satisfactory, a set of procedures which is clearly signalled and is clearly different from standard practices for everyone else.*

4. *Administrators play a more significant role in teachers' staff development. To do this they need to continue gaining skills as observers and analysts of instruction so they can be better staff developers.*

5. *Teachers play a more significant role as staff developers of each other.*

Therefore we are forming a joint committee of teachers and administrators to examine what we do each year of the four-year cycle. We are asking them to come up with a plan that will meet the state law in such a way as to accomplish the five outcomes above. We already do evaluation; this is a chance to create a "Professional Growth Cycle" that will do more.

The joint committee indicated in this letter was formed and consisted of all the principals (five) and teacher representatives from each building. The superintendent asked the union president to arrange for building representatives to be picked and that they be people who would be positive contributors to the process. The committee met several times through the late winter and spring. Instead of starting right in on a plan, they worked out a set of principles, or criteria by which they thought the final plan should be judged. We recommend this to our readers as a planning step. The following was their list:

Proposal of Principles

The plan for a multi-year development cycle:

1. Should make the experience of teaching more satisfying and more fun.

2. Should provide for choices, alternatives and decision-making by teachers about what they do.

3. Should require interaction with others frequently in a collaborative setting.

4. Should have as an important component a common language and conceptual system about teaching.

5. Should have activities available to study the knowledge base about teaching each year like a study group on "clarity," or a workshop on questioning techniques.

6. Should be simple and easy to manage, free from cumbersome paperwork and procedures.

7. Should be structured to have *all* participate in a meaningful way.

8. Should be thought of as a permanent continuous commitment of the district to the development of its people.

9. Should itself be evaluated periodically and be open to revision.

10. Should produce a written record of individual activities and growth at the end of each year.

11. Should involve teachers in the management and governance of structures that come out of this plan for a multi-year cycle.

12. Should encourage experimentation in one's teaching.

13. Should have adequate resources to make it work.

14. Should clearly separate administrative evaluation for job decisions from the rest of the cycle.

15. Should include a systematic way to enculturate new teachers to be constant learners.

16. Should, apart from administrative observations and evaluations, require people to receive frequent observational feedback in at least one year during the cycle about something specific in their teaching from someone knowledgeable about the thing observed for.

17. Should provide some evidence of continuity, development and growth over the years in what the district offers and what people do for their personal growth. (This implies long-range personal goal setting and planning.)

18. Should build in ways for teachers to get recognition and support for their growth, their improvements and their achievements.

The members of the Professional Growth Cycle Committee were conscientious in checking back with their faculties at each step along the way as this plan developed. In this way they got continuous input and refinement of their ideas. They also meaningfully involved faculty members and gave them a genuine sense of control in the planning process. Finally they forestalled the possibility of putting a plan on the table that would meet significant opposition when it was done. (For more on forestalling problems in decision making, see Saphier, Bigda-Peyton and Pierson, *How to Make Decisions that Stay Made* (1989).)

The committee eventually proposed a four-year cycle in which year one would be the Evaluation year. Year two was the Observation year requiring a minimum of four peer observations accompanied by preplanning and feedback. Year three was a year of Individual Choice and year four was titled the Collaboration year. In the Collaboration year teachers had to engage in some significant professional growth experience with one or more colleagues. (See Figure 5-1.) A menu of sample activities was presented for the Collaboration, Individual Choice and Observation years,. (See Appendix J.)

Other school districts where we have worked have come up with other configurations to accomplish the ends of the four-year cycle described above. In one school district the secondary teachers were evaluated by housemasters and principals and the supervision and observation was conducted by department heads. There are many configurations possible to increase the frequency and potency of observational feedback to teachers, but central to all of them is having in place, as mentioned before, 1) the time and resources, 2) focus, 3) attitudes, 4) training and 5) expectations necessary to make them work.

Public Teaching

"Public teaching" (Joyce 1988) means teaching within view of at least one other adult rather than in private within one's secluded four walls. The idea is that when classroom teaching is routinely public as opposed to private, it will accelerate the rate at which teachers talk about practice, learn, and improve. Practicing in public view is common in most other walks of life (Brickel 1984); its absence in teaching works against quality and against professional growth.

Routine public practice may act to elevate standards: no one wants to look bad or unprepared in front of others. But more important is the opportunity for conversation afterward about the whys and what-nexts of the teaching. Simply teaching in front of someone doesn't guarantee that these conversations will occur, but it certainly raises the odds.

When teachers team-teach with joint responsibility for the progress of a common group of children, they may teach side-by-side in the same room. This is different from other versions of teaming which have children moving between rooms and individual teachers teaching alone. The side-by-side teaming described here is close to "built in" peer observation all the time. Several dozen middle schools in Germany are so structured today. Assorted grade clusters and a few whole schools are so structured in the United States. (I myself taught in an I.G.E. school on such a team for three years—the years of fastest growth for me as a teacher.[1])

---

[1] Individually Guided Education, a model for school organization proposed and supported by the University of Wisconsin and I.D.E.A. during the late 60s, 70s and through the 80s.

FIGURE 5-1

4-Year Professional Growth Cycle

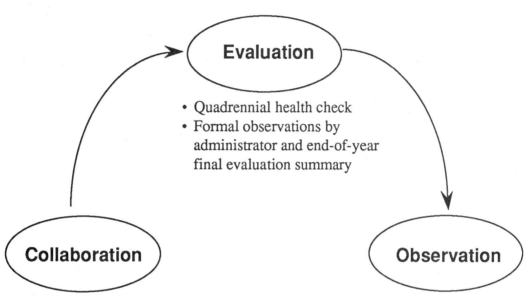

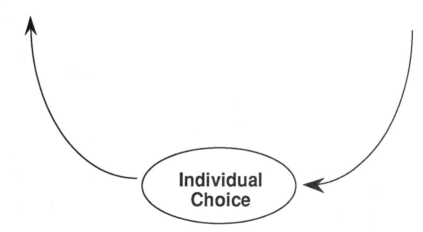

- Evaluation
  - Quadrennial health check
  - Formal observations by administrator and end-of-year final evaluation summary

- Observation
  - 4+ observations with feedback
  - Teacher selects observer
  - Teaching experiments encouraged

- Collaboration
  - Project with at least one partner, e.g.:
    - Take a course together
    - Design a course
    - Make materials
    - Co-teach

- Individual Choice
  - Read and study for classroom application
  - Curriculum design
  - Classroom teaching experiments
  - Take a course
  - Attend a study group

When you teach side-by-side with someone and have joint responsibility for children, you talk and plan together, usually daily. This talk stretches one's thinking. The two of you may have different interpretations of a child's behavior or a different opinion of what to do next with a certain lesson. Resolving these different views can lead to new insights and better decisions over time then either could have made alone. On the other hand, dividing up the subjects or the units so that each of you is really planning autonomously for your own segments encourages less professional talk and joint planning. Thus for team-teaching to be the powerful vehicle for professional growth that it can be, at least part of the time it should be co-teaching the same material at the same time with one's partner—and that, of course, creates "public teaching."

What is not built into side-by-side teaching is structured peer observation and feedback with pre and post conferences as discussed in the second section of this chapter. Were structured peer observation expected, and more, required and institutionalized on a schedule, the groupings of teachers and students for teaming described in this section would accelerate the benefits of collaborative teaching enormously.

This chapter has taken us through a progression of measures escalating in risk, but also in effect, towards making peer observations accomplish the goals of supervision we outlined in Chapter I.

- First, providing adequate time, attitudes, focus, training and expectations for peer observations, all using existing resources, could transform the experience of teaching (and increase effectiveness) for most in our profession.

- Second, multiple year evaluation cycles could institutionalize peer observations as a part of professional life. Examples of these cycles already exist.

- Third, grouping teachers and children so that two or more teachers have joint responsibility for a common group of students could create optimum conditions for fast and continuous professional learning among and between teachers, especially if linked to the systematic and continuous study of teaching.

Together and simultaneously these three conditions could create an attractive, growth oriented environment for adults that would attract and keep excellent and motivated young people in the profession of teaching[1] and elevate experienced people to new heights of effectiveness.

---

[1] We currently lose in their first five years of teaching 80% of those who scored in the top 80% of their classes in college.

VI.
Conclusion

CONCLUSION

In this monograph we advanced the theme that supervision and evaluation influence the culture of the whole institution. *How* we do supervision and evaluation sends strong messages about "how it will be around here" on all 12 norms of school culture described at the beginning of Chapter V and is intimately connected with whether or not the school will, indeed, foster constant learning among adults as well as students. Evaluation is an everyday, on-going practice, found in some form in all schools. Elsewhere (Saphier and King, 85) we have claimed that strong school cultures are built through everyday contacts among adults as they conduct the regular business of school life. This continues to be true; but because evaluation bears so directly on job security and on teachers' self-esteem, so directly on teachers' sense of control of their destiny, it is crucial for school culture builders to understand how to channel all that energy in positive directions.

We have argued that "making supervision and evaluation really work" means, in reality, accomplishing nine different important outcomes. We have argued that being clear about those outcomes focuses us on making observation and feedback productive in different ways; and when we are clear about our purposes for observation we can meaningfully define and differentiate supervision and evaluation.

It may have struck the reader that the proposals in this monograph have the effect of separating supervision and evaluation quite dramatically. We have, in effect, defined supervision and evaluation differently and gone about designing systems and procedures for accomplishing the different goals of the two. Consider the following as bottom line statements of purpose:

The purpose of evaluation is to maintain high, minimum standards of performance.

The purpose of supervision is to provide frequent, high-quality feedback by someone who knows what he/she is talking about for the purpose of stimulating teachers' thinking about teaching decisions.

The purposes of evaluation, then, become simpler. Evaluation is like an annual (or tri-annual) health check. It is not intended to be a primary vehicle for professional development—though in the hands of a skilled administrator and a reflective teacher, *any* observation with feedback is an opportunity for learning. By and large, evaluation will aim to protect students from low performing teachers by identifying them and kicking in intensive procedures for help. Evaluation defines the floor below which performance is not acceptable and insures the organization against perpetuating bad practice in teaching. More should not be expected, given the span of control of most administrators (20 to 50 teachers); and accomplishing this much well will be significant.

Supervision, however, is where we should concentrate our time and our resources. It is true that administrators in schools as they are currently configured cannot provide frequent feedback and participate in reflective discourse often enough with teachers. But, for that matter, neither can teachers with each other!

We can take care of the requirements of good evaluation as defined above with the personnel and the resources we currently have if we make the adjustments recommended in this monograph—which include narrowing our expectations for what teacher evaluation is supposed to accomplish. But arranging for good supervision, where the goal is to develop systematic activities that embed feedback, stimulation, and reflection for teachers is harder. We have shown how it is possible with a well thought-out four-year professional growth cycle as described in the last section and in Appendix J. But we also know that simultaneously it is essential for leaders to strengthen the twelve cultural norms described in Chapter V because they all contribute to a growth-oriented, satisfying workplace for adults.

Throughout this monograph and through our years of working with teachers and administrators to improve supervision and evaluation, the school culture framework has been the background and ultimate measuring stick of success. How does the way we do supervision and evaluation influence the overall culture of the school?

The approaches recommended here influence culture directly in several ways. First, when evaluation is taken seriously and poor teaching is addressed directly, everyone—staff, parents, community—feels pride in being a part of the school system. It is not an ebullient, slap-ourselves-on-the-back kind of pride. It is a quiet sense that we have high standards of performance for people who work with our children, and we will do what we have to to maintain quality instruction for all. Administrators who take on the hard job of documenting poor teaching and working with such individuals will not receive hugs of thanks or parties of appreciation for those acts. But they should know that their staff is silently grateful somebody finally had the guts and the insight to do something; and they are proud to be a member of an institution that has high standards.

Second, all the *other* procedures and practices we have within the systems we call supervision and evaluation—procedures and practices that have nothing to do with unsatisfactory teaching—are powerful vehicles for showing whether or not we are really committed to professional growth, feedback, and reflection in our professional environment. They may obstruct, ignore, or facilitate the growth of such an environment.

When viewed from within the school culture framework, evaluation and especially supervision become key systems for school improvement because they are the systems (perhaps one could add hiring) that focus on the *people* in the organization. If we are to enter the 21st century with constantly improving schools, we must focus our resources on our people, on increasing their knowledge, skill, and commitment to the learning of all children. Work on curriculum, facilities, funding, governance and other such issues will continue to be vital. But where the rubber meets the road in our business is what happens between teachers and children, day to day, lesson to lesson, minute to minute. Nothing else will matter if we do not create conditions for high performance and constant learning by those who work directly with our children; supervision and evaluation are the gates through which we must pass to create those conditions. Therefore we must do it well.

References

REFERENCES

Brickell, H. (1984, March). Address at A.S.C.D. Convention, New York.

Brophy, J. (1979, Spring). "Praise: A Functional Analysis." *Review of Educational Research*, 51/1, pp. 5-32.

Cohen, D. K. and R.J. Murnane (1985, Summer). "The Merits of Merit Pay." *The Public Interest,* Washington, D.C.: National Affairs, Inc., Vol. 80, pp. 3-30.

Costa, A. and R. Garmston (1990). *The Art of Cognitive Coaching: Supervision for Intelligent Teaching.* Training Syllabus, Sacramento, CA: Institute for Intelligent Behavior.

Costa, A. (1991). *Supervision for Intelligent Teaching.* Sacramento, CA: Search Models Unlimited.

Costa, A. and R. Garmston (1992, Spring). "Cognitive Coaching: A Strategy for Reflective Teaching," *Journal for Supervision and Curriculum Improvement.* Place, CA: Association for Supervision and Curriculum Development.

Devaney, K. (1987, March). *The Lead Teacher: Ways to Begin.* New York: The Carnegie Forum on Education and the Economy.

Duke, D.L. and R.J. Stiggins (1990). "Beyond Minimum Compentence: Evaluation for Professional Development." J. Millman and L. Darling-Hammond, eds. *Teacher Evaluation.* Newbury Park, CA: Sage.

Gabor, A. (1990). *The Man Who Discovered Quality.* New York: Random House.

Glassie, H. (1982). *Passing the Time in Ballymenone.* Philadelphia: University of Pennsylvania Press.

Joyce, B. and B. Showers (1988). *Student Achievement Through Staff Development.* New York: Longman.

Lieberman, A., ed., (1988). *Building a Professional Culture in Schools.* New York: Teachers College Press.

Lieberman, A. and A. Miller (1979). *Staff Development, New Demands, New Realities, New Perspectives.* New York: Teachers College Press.

Little, J.W. (1982, Fall). "Norms of Collegiality and Experimentation: Workplace Conditions of School Success." *American Educational Research Journal*, 19/3, pp. 325-340.

Natriello, G. (1984, Fall). "Teachers' Perceptions of the Frequency of Evaluation and Assessments of Their Effort and Effectiveness." *American Educational Research Journal*, 21/3, pp. 579-595.

Saphier, J. T. Bigda-Peyton and G. Pierson (1989). *How to Make Decisions That Stay Made*. Carlisle, MA: Research for Better Teaching.

Saphier, J. and R. Gower (1987). *The Skillful Teacher*. Carlisle, MA: Research for Better Teaching.

Saphier, J. and M. King (1985, March). "Good Seeds Grow in Strong Cultures." *Educational Leadership*.

Sarason, S. (1982, 2nd edition). *The Culture of the School and the Problem of Change*. New York: Allyn and Bacon.

Schlecty, P. (1986, March). Address, A.S.C.D. Convention. San Francisco.

Zahorik, J.A. "Teachers Collegial Interaction: An Exploratory Study," *The Elementary School Journal*. 87, pp. 385-396.

APPENDIX A

■

Criteria for Effective Teaching
(sample from one district)

CRITERIA FOR EFFECTIVE TEACHING

I.   TEACHING TECHNIQUES
II. TEACHER-STUDENT RELATIONSHIPS
III. PROFESSIONAL RESPONSIBILITIES
IV. STAFF RELATIONSHIPS

I. TEACHING TECHNIQUES

The primary role of the teacher is that of director of learning. The teacher must plan, implement and evaluate programs which facilitate learning.

The following are parameters and examples that might be considered in meeting this criteria. They are not meant as a checklist.

A. Maintains attention.
  1. Maximizes time on task.
  2. Uses suitable moves to get attention.

B. Maintains momentum of lesson.
  1. Provides materials for lesson.
  2. Able to manage two or more groups.
  3. Handles intrusions with a minimum of disruption to the flow of the lesson.
  4. Anticipates trouble spots.
  5. Is flexible in presentation if difficulty develops.
  6. Prepares students for transitions.

C. Communicates expectations.
  1. Provides adequately for quantity and quality of work.
  2. Informs students of expectations for performance and learning with a positive expectancy.
  3. Gives prompt and appropriate feedback.
  4. Maintains high standards.

D. Plans and communicates procedural routines.
  1. Addresses housekeeping routines.
  2. Communicates work habits and work procedures.

E. Demonstrates clarity of presentation.
  1. Checks and probes for understanding.
  2. Tries to unscramble confusions.
  3. Uses a variety of explanatory devices and techniques.
  4. Speech is appropriate.
  5. States objectives of lessons.
  6. Provides for linkage between ideas.
  7. Summarizes the lesson.

F. Appropriately uses teaching strategies known to be effective in enhancing learning. (Ex., The principles of learning outlined in Chapter 9 of *The Skillful Teacher*).

G. Demonstrates efficient use of time and space.
   1. Provides enough time to learn the skill.
   2. Provides sufficient interactive time with pupils.
   3. Focuses on beginning and ending time.
   4. Arranges space to suit learning activity when permitted.
   5. Teaches for mastery when appropriate.

H. Appropriately utilizes a variety of teaching models such as direct instruction, group investigation, awareness training, development of inductive thinking, inquiry training, advanced organization of information, etc. (Some of the models of teaching which would be applicable are outlined in Chapter 12 of *The Skillful Teacher*.)

I. Uses appropriate objectives in the lesson.

J. Evaluates student progress.
   1. Checks student progress through observations, work samples, tests, interviews and/or student self-evaluation.
   2. Matches test to what is taught.
   3. Indicates criteria for success to students.
   4. Provides quick and candid feedback.
   5. Maintains well organized records.
   6. When appropriate repeats evaluation at future date to assess permanence of learning.

II. TEACHER—STUDENT RELATIONSHIPS
   The teacher should recognize that a student's emotional development directly affects his/her academic growth. A teacher, therefore, should respond to a student's emotional and social needs to facilitate that growth.
   The following are areas and examples that might be considered in meeting this criteria:

A. Recognizes the student as an individual.
   1. Maintains effective communications with students.
   2. Works to establish good rapport with students.
   3. Uses students' previous and current teachers as resources where appropriate.
   4. Helps student increase his/her self-image.
   5. Helps students establish realistic goals.
   6. Helps students develop a sense of responsibility and self-discipline.
   7. Communicates high expectations in performance and behavior.
   8. Is available for individual work with students.
   9. Counsels students.

B. Helps the student develop as a group member.
  1. Helps each student interact effectively in groups.
  2. Helps student adapt to and socialize within classroom environment.
  3. Creates classroom atmosphere which encourages acceptance of others' rights to have different attitudes and values.
  4. Helps student recognize value of his/her own uniqueness.
  5. Demonstrates and encourages respect for all cultures, races and religions.

C. Possesses the following traits which engender student respect.
  1. Is fair.
  2. Presents a professional appearance.
  3. Has a sense of humor.
  4. Is courteous.
  5. Shows respect.
  6. Listens attentively.

D. Communicates and maintains standards for discipline through a positive approach.
  1. Is direct.
  2. Is specific.
  3. Repeats those standards.
  4. Has positive expectancy.
  5. Upholds standards consistently.
  6. Has tenacity.
  7. Employs a variety of strategies matched to the situation.

III. PROFESSIONAL RESPONSIBILITIES

The competent teacher has a responsibility to seek improvement in professional self-growth, in the school system, and in the teaching profession, and to foster positive and effective relationships with parents.

The following are areas and examples that might be considered in meeting this criteria:

A. Keeps abreast of current professional training: i.e., course work, in-service work, conferences, membership in professional organizations, professional reading, etc.

B. Considers suggestions from supervisors, peers, students and parents.

C. Carries out the educational goals of the system.

D. Assists others in the profession when the opportunity arises.

E. Actively contributes to the enhancement and improvement of the _____Public Schools through consistent participation in some activity/ies such as:
  • sharing in the development of the overall programs objectives and policies of the school or school system

- participating in the formulation and development of the curriculum for the school system
- involvement in the leadership of the _____ Teachers Association
- attendance at athletic and musical events/chaperoning dances and/or other student social activities; organization and/or management of such student social activities
- involvement in teacher councils and/or other advisory groups
- participation in orientation meetings for parents and/or other information sessions for the public.

F. Maintains a record for attendance and punctuality which reflects a strong commitment to teaching.

G. Submits reports and required materials on time.

H. Encourages and initiates parent conferences when appropriate.

I. Answers communication from parents as promptly as possible.

J. Supports parent-teacher groups.

K. Informs parents and public about school activities when appropriate.

L. Utilizes available community resources when appropriate.

IV. STAFF RELATIONSHIPS

The responsibilities of a teacher are broader and more inclusive than teaching a specific subject or grade level. As a member of the total school community the teacher should share the responsibilities for accomplishing the objectives of the school and for cooperating with other staff members toward that end.

The following are areas and examples that might be considered in meeting this criteria:

A. Shares the responsibilities for the supervision of students outside the classroom during the school day.

B. Shares ideas, suggestions and resources with others.

C. Attempts to promote good relationships with the staff.

D. Shares the responsibility to participate in school and system-wide activities with colleagues.

E. Is positive and supportive of colleagues and the school system with the public.

F. Cooperates when possible with reasonable requests made by administration.

G. Works effectively with Pupil Support Services.

H. Seeks to maintain effective working relationship with all school system personnel.

APPENDIX B

■

Sample Classroom Observation Write-ups

Observation of *Dorothy Ames*

High School   **A.P. English**

Dorothy began the class by handing out a compilation of the students' suggested essay questions for *Crime and Punishment* and their ideas about what makes a good answer to an essay question. This activity (the writing and sharing) helped to activate the students' current knowledge, first for this period's discussion about the novel and second, for the following day's in-class practice essay writing assignment. This was an excellent writing-to-learn activity in that it prepared each student to do the kind of thinking needed to produce effective discussion and essays.

There were two intrusions to the class early in the period. One girl came in late, a bag of ice tied to her ankle indicating that she had an injury. Dorothy greeted her and acknowledged her situation by moving a second chair over to her to let her elevate her foot. The other students were busy reading over each others' ideas, so there was no break in the momentum of the class. Dorothy handled another intrusion, a student question ("What do you need now?" "Scissors" "In the top drawer"), very quickly, again maintaining the class' momentum.

As the students commented on their own questions and suggestions, Dorothy showed resemblance to something (a way of thinking about characters) the students already knew. "I've noticed you've changed your opinions of some of the characters as you get to know them better," and later, "I was hoping you would bring out the characters [in your questions] and you did. I'd like to focus on that today in part 6." This was one way that she prepared the students for their small group discussion work that followed.

Some students had finished reading the novel and others had not. Dorothy anticipated confusion because of this and warned the students to be careful to discuss only the assigned chapter in their small groups. As an explanatory device, Dorothy had written the characters' names on the board and referred to them while she stated the assignment for each small group: to come to some conclusion about what they now knew, after having read this section of the novel, about a specific character.

Dorothy elicited active student participation by breaking the class into 3 small discussion groups of 4 students each and assigning a recorder for each group. Dorothy listened briefly to the first group and decided that they and the other groups needed the directions repeated. She then explained the assignment to each separate group, clarifying and highlighting important ideas ("Yesterday, you gave me a lot of the ways people felt about X. Perhaps reading chapters 3 and 4 has changed, reinforced, negated your ideas about him. For example, you may feel he is *more likely to...*"). This re-explaining to each group was not an efficient use of Dorothy's or the students' time. Although Dorothy had helped the students prepare for the assignment (see evidence above for showing resemblance and anticipating confusion), she could have taken additional steps to help them—for example, checking for understanding of the assignment more thoroughly and eliciting examples of well-supported conclusions from the students—before the class broke into groups. In addition, I would suggest giving students advance notice for this type of assignment so they can focus their reading and thinking the night before.

As the groups worked together, Dorothy gave them notice about the time they had ("Two minutes!"). She circulated among the groups again, helping them to reach their conclusions by asking comprehension questions ("Do you believe that? Why? Do you have enough evidence right now?") and keeping a clear focus of questions ("Do you admire that honesty? Why not? Why not give him that benefit? Any saving graces at all?") This questioning helped the students see if they had reasons to support their conclusions about the characters.

Dorothy brought the students back to the large group using humor and enthusiasm: "This is going to be fun. I know you are feeling passionate about these people and have violent opinions."

A.P. English 12, by definition, demands that students cover a good deal of material and engage in constant higher-level thinking. Dorothy used writing-to-learn and small group discussion work to activate the students' knowledge and to keep them thinking; these are very good, efficient strategies. I suggest that Dorothy check for understanding and unscramble confusions earlier on in the class so that the students will be able to use class time even more efficiently and effectively.

Observation of *Dick Lauren*

High School   **Special Ed Science**

Observation took place during a science lesson with six high school students present. The lesson was broken down into three parts and taught using a teacher-directed total class format. Mr. Lauren taught from the front of the class and from in front of the group when they were outside.

During the first part of the lesson in the classroom which lasted twelve minutes, Mr. Lauren introduced and discussed sunspots with the class. The second part of the lesson, which lasted ten minutes, consisted of an experiment outside in which the group tried to get sunspots on a piece of paper through a pinhole technique. Lastly, the class returned to the room and had another discussion of sunspots and other topics before being dismissed.

Mr. Lauren exhibited positive personal relationships with his students which helped make them feel more comfortable and diffused potential altercations between students. When one student, who had not been in class due to a suspension, arrived, Mr. Lauren stated, "Welcome back, nice seeing you. Nice haircut; it looks pretty good." Additionally when one youngster made a joke and another laughed at him, Mr. Lauren utilized humor first and then stated, "J.J., you know John's sense of humor." These interactions were clearly beneficial and are Mr. Lauren's strength.

There appeared to be no specific expectations for behaviors such as feet on the desk, calling out and interrupting either the teacher or other students when they were talking or staying on task. When a student had his feet on the desk, no intervention took place. Further, when the student leaned back and fell over as a result of this position, no intervention took place either.

Throughout the lesson, students constantly called out and interrupted Mr. Lauren's lesson. While some of the call-outs were on topic, many were not. Mr. Lauren in every case responded to the interruption with feedback about the content of the comment and not once gave the students a clear expectation that they should wait to be called on or stay on topic. During his discussion of the temperature of the sun, John called out, "There's got to be life forms in other places in the galaxy," to which Mr. Lauren responded, "Maybe." The next few minutes were taken up with a calling out debate among students as to whether life forms existed or not. The topic of sunspots was lost in the exchange.

Additionally, there was no evidence of posted rules or expectations in the class. The lack of specific behavioral expectations hampered Mr. Lauren's objectives of keeping students on task during the lesson and mastering the content knowledge about sunspots by consistently breaking the momentum of instruction.

There was also little evidence in the lesson of adequate planning on Mr. Lauren's part. First, even though he provided the students with information that in 10% of the cases the experiment designed to produce a sunspot might not work, Mr. Lauren did not tell the students why, and when asked directly by one student, responded, "I don't know enough about it; I'll check it out and tell you tomorrow." After the experiment failed to produce the sunspots and his aide asked, "What kind of paper should you use?" he responded in front of the students, "I used the thing that was the handiest; it doesn't say what kind of paper." This lack of preparation and lack of knowledge of content inhibited the learning process for the students and even frustrated one of them who was motivated by the interesting topic.

Finally, Mr. Lauren's objectives regarding what sunspots are and why we should study them was never addressed completely in the lesson. The students were never instructed in the important content material and as such, could never answer any of the questions asked by Mr. Lauren such as, "If you saw those black spots, what would you assume they're from?"

An on-task log was kept by the observer for a brief five minute period to assess whether the students were paying attention to the lesson. Evidence from the log revealed that Julie, who was not seated directly in front of Mr. Lauren was off task for three minutes and fifteen seconds of the five minute period. No attempt to engage her in the lesson took place by Mr. Lauren.

In conclusion, Mr. Lauren, while exhibiting personal relationship skills which had a positive effect on motivation and management, failed to exhibit the planning and instructional skills which would have enabled the students to reach the content objectives for this science class.

Recommendations:

Dick, the following recommendations are being offered to help upgrade the level of instruction in your classroom and meet your objectives for students:

Behavioral Expectations
Develop specific behavioral expectations and rules with your class. The rules should be consistent with rules in the other classrooms and should be stated in positive ways rather than "Don'ts". The rules need to be reviewed with the students both during the process and periodically thereafter. They should be posted and should include behaviors that facilitate the instructional process. These should include

such things as students respecting the rights of others including yourself by not interrupting, and students staying on topic during discussions.

Both Ray and I will be available to help you formulate the rules should you request that help. I would like these developed by the first day of school after the holiday vacation and handed in to me no later than that date.

Planning

Your lesson planning needs to be more detailed so that you can insure that you won't get sidetracked from the content you want students to master and so that you can answer student questions adequately. For each lesson as part of the curriculum, you should include the following in written form:

a. specific objective(s),
b. an outline of the procedures you will use during the lesson,
c. the materials necessary to complete the lesson,
d. the content that needs to be mastered, and
e. how you will evaluate student mastery.

Methodology

Describe the objectives and activities for the class at the beginning of the lesson and summarize the material at the end of the lesson. Explicitly include important content material on the board or in a handout or verbally at some point in the lesson.

Review important experiments before the lesson to insure that they will work.

Make sure that all students are engaged in the lesson by using one or more of the following instructional strategies: (1) calling on them to answer questions periodically to assess whether they were listening; (2) physically going over to them and standing nearby for a short period; and/or (3) turning toward the particular student while presenting the lesson.

I'm sure that increasing both the behavioral expectations and the planning components of instruction will result in an instructional climate that will increase mastery learning in your classes.

Observation of *Eleanor Halliday*

Grade 2   **Speech & Language**

Eleanor Halliday is a speech and language teacher who was observed teaching a language lesson to a second grade class on January 4.

She set the stage for learning by having all her materials together as she entered the room. Notice was given to the students as she walked in, "Hi, finish drinks and get settled for language" so that they knew what was about to occur. She anticipated distraction of an observer by introducing me to the class. "This is Mrs. Eliot. She is here to listen to our lesson." Her standards for speech class were reviewed prior to beginning the lesson by stating, "Let's review the speech rules." As students answered, "Don't talk out, don't pinch, quiet hands, good sitting, don't goof around," it was clear that they knew what was expected behavior during "Speech time." Her objective for the class was clear. "We are comparing things today." She was able to activate prior knowledge by asking, "Who knows what this means?" Brendan's quick answer, "Draw between one to another, I mean same and different," focused the class on the key learning words.

Eleanor began the formal lesson by telling the class what the objective was, "We will begin by comparing a dog and a cat (writing on board: *dog cat*). I'll draw a bridge between the two when you tell me what is the same." She was encouraging to the students as they answered with comments such as "That's a good one." "Good one, Mark." "That's a really good one." This shows her ability to encourage all her students to participate.

When Elizabeth, who had raised her hand was called on and then drew a blank, Eleanor responded, "You want to think a few minutes more?" she then turned to the class and continued with "let's go over this together." The signal at first seemed to be that she would come back to Elizabeth after she'd had time to think about it, but then Eleanor explained the item to the class. This got Elizabeth off the hook, but denied her the chance to think through the example. The shift to the class left Elizabeth with her own thoughts; encouraging Elizabeth to answer might have kept her more focused on the lesson and communicated positive expectations.

Eleanor next turned to the board and pointed to the word "legs". She asked, "Can you give me sentences with this word, David?" David was not able to answer, so she gave him a cue. "Remember, I said dogs and cats both have four paws." He quickly added, "Dogs and cats have four paws and four legs." In this way, he was able to experience success.

Eleanor made a smooth transition to "different" from "same" by saying, "Last one …they're both animals…good. Now let's see how they are different." When given the answer, "Dogs smell and cats don't", she unscrambled confusion by having the student explain his own thinking. She said, "Tell me more about that." This allowed her the opportunity to understand what the student was really thinking. His answer that dogs can track smells was on target and was validated by her decision not to assume an incorrect answer, but to explore it more fully.

When Elizabeth offered, "Dogs are brown, a cat isn't.", Eleanor continued the questioning with, "Are all dogs brown? Think of another one." With no answer from Elizabeth, she added, "That was good trying." As Elizabeth placed her head on the desk, facing away from the teacher, it was clear that she got the message…good trying, but not good answer. Changing the expectations for Elizabeth might give very different results. If the expectation was that "You can do it", Elizabeth might have persevered.

Eleanor made a transition between activities easy for the students. She gave an itinerary for the activity change. "We are going to work with a partner. Now each of you will be telling two things that are the same about each other and two things that are different. I will give you partners, then find a quiet corner in the room. You will have five minutes." This activity was also a good change of pace for these second graders by allowing them some structured movement away from desk work.

Once the five minutes were up, she smoothed the transition with, "Okay, we are ready, everyone quiet . . . . (wait time). All right, back in your seats and together."

As the class began to listen to the partners reporting to the group on sameness and differences, a general restlessness was noted. Eleanor was able to refocus the group with both directed and general comments, "Tommy, listen carefully, because I'm going to ask you one thing that is the same about David and Dawn," and "Remember, we need quiet sitting".

Eleanor ended the class by helping them to see the many times they make comparisons, eliciting examples from the class to be sure they understood the concept.

Observation of *Jim Lynch*

Grade 11   **Curriculum I English**

I observed Jim's Lynch's junior Curriculum I English class on February 28, 1990. Jim had the students study in detail two brief excerpts, one from Benjamin Franklin's *Autobiography* and another from Jonathon Edwards' *Religious Affections* in order to prepare them for a later reading and analysis of the Declaration of Independence. During this class Jim demonstrated many effective teacher strategies; his ability to get the students to follow the lesson was impressive, even extraordinary. He showed concern for his students' needs and individual differences, but he did not give them adequate time or opportunity to voice their response to or comprehension of the material.

Jim began the class with a brief discussion of the courses the students might elect for their English classes during the senior year. He reminded them that they would have many distractions during the senior year such as cars and the prom, but that they should think clearly about the academic issues of the senior year now. He told them that they should not get to college and discover that they had missed out on reading the books that their classmates had. He urged them to take the courses with a lot of reading and ended this part of the discussion by saying, "You need to do a little self-assessment. Ask yourself, 'what is it that I need?" This presentation established that he cared about the students' choices, understood the demands and distractions of the senior year and that the selection of English courses was important business.

Fifteen minutes into the class Jim passed out the photocopied sheets containing the two passages to be studied and reminded the class that this lesson was preparing them for their study the next day of the content and prose style of the Declaration of Independence. He asked two different students to read aloud the long paragraph by Franklin and requested that the students underline words that they did not know. After two students had contributed one word each, no more hands were raised. Jim called on a black student named Demone and asked him what "unprovoked" meant. Demone said, "I know what it means, but I can't explain it." Jim stayed with him until he <u>had</u> explained it by giving him some progressive minimal cues. He did not permit the student to get away with saying, "I can't…".

In this and other interactions Jim appeared to know what he could get from each individual student. He involved many students in the process of running through the readings. He constantly checked to see if they were following, sometimes asking for something as simple as the word that completed the sentence he was reading, other times posing a question which required an understanding of the meaning of the passage, but in all cases making certain that the students' heads were into the passages. All appeared to be paying attention throughout the lesson. He moved rapidly from one student to the next and most responded quickly enough so that momentum was maintained throughout. Jim is a master at moving his students through the material and maintaining their attention as well as knowing which students are capable of what responses.

Jim uses emotion and personal anecdotes to keep the students' attention. He mentioned his daughters' fighting over a doll to reinforce a point on how people will fight to attain and retain what they desire in life, even at the expense of others. At other times, he asked how many students had pets and why might someone become a vegetarian to reinforce a point Franklin makes about giving up his own vegetarianism when he was hungry and fresh cod was being cooked. Jim varies the tone and volume of his voice throughout and dramatizes his points constantly. He expends enormous energy and affect.

Both of the readings were presented in the context of a Puritan-Yankee-Romantic continuum which Jim had written on the board and the class had obviously discussed earlier. Jim appeared to be preparing the students for the tension between the rational and romantic elements which they will encounter in the Declaration of Independence. Jim's classes have a serious and intellectual tone. He has the students read difficult works from William Bradford to John Donne to William Shakespeare. Jim takes American literature very seriously and expects his students to do likewise, as is evidenced by many direct remarks: "This is hard material, but you will all be able to master it with effort. It's giving you a sense of how ideas influence history that you'll be able to use throughout your life—from understanding events in the news to planning your own future."

Despite Jim's constant interaction with many of his students, no student said more than twenty or thirty words at a time. For the most part students were expected to supply short answers and Jim would supply all the rest. There were Jim's anecdotes, Jim's emotions, Jim's energy, Jim's questions and often Jim's answer. At no time did a student respond to any point that another student had made.

In a post-class conference I told Jim that the class was like a trolley driven by Jim. The students had their individualized hand-holds and Jim was careful that all were hanging on as the trolley moved swiftly down the tracks, but it was difficult to tell what the students had truly contributed or retained. There were impressive pictures outside the windows as the trolley moved along, but the students were not able to interact with any of the material on *their* terms.

I urged Jim, who is a master teacher at moving kids through and exposing them to material, to give his students more of a voice in the classroom both through more open discussion of the issues in the literature and through shared writing assignments where students could give personalized responses in their own voice to the issues at hand. Student opinions and responses should be shared, valued, even criticized under the controlled conditions of the classroom.

Jim showed me one assignment in which students write a response to the Declaration of Independence as if they were a British staff officer reporting the contents of the document to a superior. Later he was extremely pleased at the essays this particular class wrote on the topic. Such an assignment moves in the direction of giving the students more voice and Jim should continue to develop ways of permitting and encouraging students to participate in more substantial ways in his classroom.

There were scores of examples of excellent teaching to be pointed out in this particular class and I applaud Jim for all of them. At the same time I am convinced that his teaching would be more effective and his students would feel more fulfilled if they were given more of a voice.

Observation of *JoAnne Venice*

Grade 5   **Mathematics**

This grade 5 math class was in progress when the observer arrived at 8:52 a.m. The classroom was set up to provide students with a very comfortable learning environment. There were a variety of science-related posters and exhibits on display as well as math papers from several classes. The classroom space was well organized with 22 of the students divided into four subgroups at clustered tables.

The remedial math group, which included three students, was working at the back of the room. The objective for that group was to practice two-digit whole number multiplication. The students were allowed to use a multiplication grid for the number facts of which they were unsure and they were encouraged to check their products with an answer sheet. Thus, Mrs. Venice was able to ensure that the students were practicing their number facts correctly and they were able to get immediate feedback as to the accuracy of their multiplication.

The momentum of the class was excellent. Mrs. Venice never "missed a beat" when she encountered an intrusion. "Laura," she said softly, "you know when I leave papers turned upside down you are not to touch them." In addition to the materials required for the remedial group, the remaining groups were given three decks of decimal cards and scratch paper. Halfway through the lesson, Mrs. Venice distributed teacher-prepared decimal squares in precounted stacks. She left them in the corner of each group table. Therefore, the momentum of the class was never broken for lack of materials because students never had to leave their seats for any reason.

Mrs. Venice's instructions were very clear. At the start of the lesson, she reviewed the significance of the colors of the cards (red - tenths; green - hundredths; yellow - thousandths). She was able to quickly read facial cues showing puzzlement and, through a series of specific questions, she was able to pinpoint areas of confusion. "What was the *second* word in my instructions?" ("Red") "That's right! Now once again, find two squares representing seven-tenths each and put them side by side." Students demonstrated their understanding by completing the task quickly. "Let me show you this on a number line on the overhead," was also a good clarity move. The use of the overhead projector focused all attention on the problem and served to provide another concrete method of illustrating that 2 x .7 = 1.4. Observing some confusion about how to express amounts greater than one whole, Mrs. Venice demonstrated flexibility. "Let's try an easier one. Find two squares equal to four tenths. Put them side by side. Kathy, what example does that illustrate?" (Two times .4 equals .8.) "Good, now let's see your cards." Kathy held up her cards and correctly overlapped the first card onto the second illustrating eight tenths. In this way, Mrs.

Venice offered reassurance and an opportunity for all students to check their understanding in a non-threatening tone.

This lesson employed several principles of learning. One involved the planning of a sequence of activities from concrete to abstract. This was clearly illustrated in the tasks involved with the decimal cards, the number line, the shading of decimal squares by the students individually, to the final activity of writing decimal number statements with the correct product without the use of any concrete materials. Active participation was another key in this lesson. Whether choosing the correct decimal cards, shading their individual cards, illustrating examples on the overhead number line, or serving as a checker for their group, the students were discussing, comparing, as well as practicing multiplication of decimals.

Attention moves by Mrs. Venice were very effective. "All eyes on me." "Time Out - Freeze!" illustrated examples where Mrs. Venice demanded and received, in a pleasant manner, the immediate attention of all four groups. Individual students, as well as groups, received praise and encouragement. "Good job, Kathy!!" "I like the way you wrote that out, Jason!" "This group did a very good job on that one!" "Which group will be the first to complete the next example," inserted an element of competition which students obviously enjoyed.

Special note should be made of Mrs. Venice's ability to overlap two lessons. While a greater amount of instructional time was spent with the decimal groups, Mrs. Venice made it a point to connect with the remedial group several times as she moved around the room checking students. "That's very good work," served to bolster the remedial students and served to reassure them that they were an important part of the class, although they were doing other tasks.

In summary, this was a well-paced, creative and challenging lesson. Students were actively involved in the learning process and demonstrated a keen interest in the objectives of the lesson. Mrs. Venice is to be commended for her fine work.

Observation of *Kathleen Sutton*

Grade 5   **Mathematics**

Observation took place during grade 5 math class. This included a short review of some material previously covered (e.g., commutative, associative laws, ancient Egyptian number system), some word problems from the text on distances and a brief presentation of "Annexing" zeros in multiplication before students worked on some problems which involved annexing.

Starting off with a brief review of material previously covered provided an opportunity for reinforcing the concepts and for helping the understanding of students who might not have previously been clear about it. After eliciting a few students' responses to the question of "What's wrong with the ancient Egyptians' math system?", you provided a verbal summary ("Remember—no zero, no place value, didn't lend itself to multiplication and division"). This summarizing helps students' understanding. It could have been enhanced by also writing it to provide visual as well as auditory input.

Unfortunately, there was little, if any, evidence of checking on students' understanding during the bulk of the period. While you did tell students as they worked on problems that "anybody having any trouble, just raise your hand", this only helps those students who realize they're having trouble and who then ask for help. At one point, Michelle put her hand down after having it up for a while without your seeing it. One way to provide more effective instruction would be for you to circulate and closely observe students actually working out problems so that you can pick up on and correct errors as a student makes them. Also, in responding to students' questions, asking them how they *think* they might proceed allows them to try to figure it out and also lets you know more about their understanding than does your telling them what to do. (E.g. with Emily, you told her, "Here's Yosemite, here's Grand Canyon… so subtract smaller from larger". With Khalfani, you read the instructions for him and added, "that means either travel that route or this route".) In going over the answers, your question of "how many had that (correct answer)?" did not enable those who did *not* have the correct answer to figure out or understand *why* their answers were wrong. In one instance, Mike M. attempted on his own to find out where he'd gone wrong, after which he told you, "I had ___ instead of ___". Your response of "Okay" did not validate the fact that he'd figured out the *reason* for his incorrect answer—an important aspect of learning. This sort of figuring out should be regularly encouraged. Having students paired up or grouped in order to agree on correct answers would help force them to rework problems until they could reach agreement.

At one point when students were working on the radio announcer problems, you provided clarification after you noticed "some are getting confused by the problem 15 X 850". You proceeded to write the example on the board. Although I do not think this particular example indicated the advantage of annexing zeros (since annexing isn't much shorter than conventional multiplication), the attempt to pick up on common confusions and clarify them should be continued. You also gave one good visual clue (drawing of house and annex) to help students figure out the term "annexing".

During the whole period, there were a number of students (e.g. Allison, Debbie, Jesse, Kristina, Hana, Lori, Pam) who were never called upon, never asked questions, nor ever interacted with you. Therefore, I would think it difficult to assess their understanding of the material.

In the future, I would expect to see more effective means of enabling those students who are having trouble understanding a given concept or type of problem to gain greater clarity. On this occasion, I did not see sufficient evidence that this was occurring. In particular, you had no way of knowing about the many students who didn't have their hand up or volunteer to speak. As I mentioned in our post-conference, Juan or Susan are both resources you can tap to help with techniques and formats for dealing with this. They can also provide (and can come in to show use of) some of the better and more recent materials on mathematical problem-solving. The three problems on the bulletin board are examples of such, but they need to be done by students in order to have value. This is *not* to imply that word problems, such as those about the radio announcer are not important as well. Rather it's important to differentiate between problem solving that involves logical thinking, etc. and word problems which require computation. One way to help students who are having difficulty with the latter is to have them just figure out which operation(s) are required, apart from the computation itself. In this way, the task gets broken down into parts and becomes more manageable.

Observation of *Midge Garfield*

Grade 5   **Computer Lesson**

Ms. Garfield's position as K through 8 Computer Resource person is brand new this year. She visits each K-5 classroom once a month for 30-45 minutes to present new ideas and projects that support the LOGO problem solving curriculum. She returns to many classes on a request and/or random basis for shorter time periods. On these shorter "drop-in" visits she answers questions and looks at student progress. The usual physical set-up for Ms. Garfield's visit is similar to "story time"—Ms. Garfield and the computer are at the center of a half circle of sitting children.

Ms. Garfield began her lesson with a review of a concept that is a prerequisite idea for proper use of the software. She asked questions checking for comprehension and recall. "Why am I looking at RAM?" "What is RAM?" "Where is it?" "How do I get something from the disk?"

Ms. Garfield had good "wait time" between the question and calling for or taking a student response. Ms. Garfield got much of the class quickly involved in this review portion of the lesson—over half the students either volunteered responses or were called upon during this initial 10 minute discussion.

Ms. Garfield made a nice transition into the next area of her lesson—pattern recognition and using the REPEAT to make patterns in LOGO. She used her previous line of questions and responses to get a graphics pattern from disk into RAM and onto the screen for the children to observe. This served as well to demonstrate the previous review.

Ms. Garfield did not show enough variation in her style of classroom control. She would say "Sh, sh" to quiet students—the children ignored this prompt consistently. The regular classroom teacher would step in and say, "On your seat, Tim." "Say please!" "Raise your hands." "Don't call out." Ms. Garfield should try to incorporate into her own classroom management repertoire some of what she saw modeled by this classroom teacher.

Ms. Garfield is providing a learning environment in which the children's intellectual judgments are respected. Ms. Garfield inadvertently typed the word OVAL (a 4th grade command) on the screen; several students spontaneously raised their hands and/or shouted out "No! An Oval is just the letter O and numbers". Ms. Garfield smiled at her mistake and thanked them for helping her. On another occasion, Ms. Garfield didn't hide the turtle at the end of an example. The students again spoke out in firm, confident voices that "You forgot to hide the turtle!" Ms. Garfield responded, "I forgot", and then asked if anyone knew how she could do that.

Ms. Garfield encourages the "try-it" (intellectual risk taking) attitude that is fundamental to the computer curriculum. "How can I make a design come out over and over again?" was one of Ms. Garfield's queries. Ms. Garfield called on many students to get a sampling of their responses. She asked for a vote and then proceeded to do what the majority recommended. They were wrong. She asked them to observe on the screen what went wrong and to rethink their responses. Another consensus was taken with a few "why's?" thrown in and another "try-it" was done.

Ms. Garfield did not bring closure to her work with the children. This results in children not getting as much from a discussion as they might otherwise. At the end of Ms. Garfield's review of RAM, Disk, and Get, she never made time to sum these concepts up or to concisely reiterate or redefine a child's attempt at defining these ideas. At the end of class Ms. Garfield did ask if there were any questions, but she did not take this opportunity to restate the new ideas that she just spent 25 minutes exploring with the children.

Ms. Garfield didn't provide clear expectations to the children on what they were supposed to do between this visit and her return. As the lesson was ending and the class was returning to their seats, the classroom teacher politely asked Ms. Garfield to inform the class of the specific tasks that they should be preparing in anticipation of her next visit.

Ms. Garfield conducted a good lesson: she reviewed important concepts, introduced new ideas and maintained a classroom environment that was supportive of the computer curriculum's critical thinking philosophy.

During this classroom visit I observed two problem areas in Ms. Garfield's teaching. The first has to do with classroom or student management. The second deals with closure and expectations. Ms. Garfield, given her open and good rapport with the children, might try focusing on one or two of the disruptive children and say firmly but respectfully "You are disrupting the class and not giving your friends time to think up their own answers!" Ms. Garfield should plan ahead of time to sum up each major portion of her lesson and to end each lesson with a statement concerning what the children are expected to do by the time she returns.

Observation of *Phil Gerund*

High School   **Special Ed English**

The observation took place during an English class with Mr. Gerund's homeroom class of high school students. Five students were present; the teacher aide was at lunch and not present during the period. The lesson consisted of individualized vocabulary assignments with students working at their desks and Mr. Gerund circulating to each one and a teacher-directed total class word game at the end of the period.

It was clear during the observation that the students knew the routine for the class and what was expected of them during the period. All of the students came into the room after lunch, spent five minutes in quiet conversation and immediately took out their work when asked after the transition time was over. Mr. Gerund began the period by describing the activities including the word game and the reward (doughnuts) for participating during the period. This helped set the stage for the content that followed and the students responded positively to the contingencies that were announced.

Mr. Gerund exhibited high, yet well-matched expectations for his students. He individualized his instructional decisions as to when students needed help from him and was consistent and tenacious in his behavior. Adam looked at his work and without trying remarked, "I don't know 1/2 of these words". Mr. Gerund set positive expectations: "That means you know half of them, what's this one?". Mr. Gerund continued gently to support what he did know until Adam was able to be successful. By both supporting him and not giving in when he was convinced Adam had the knowledge, Mr. Gerund effectively "challenged" Adam's misbelief about his (dis)abilities which may over the long run change his behavior and feelings of inadequacy.

Throughout the lesson, Mr. Gerund used different and effective instructional strategies which were well matched to his students' needs. When Tima wanted him to tell her if the vocabulary word she selected fit the sentence, he responded, "when you're done with that one, read it back to yourself and see if it makes sense." This use of self-monitoring, rather than relying on the teacher as the first check, will help her to increase her skills and independence. A similar strategy was used with Bruce for monitoring behavior. When Mr. Gerund reminded the students of the contingencies for working, Bruce responded, "Am I working?" to which he responded, "What do you think?" Bruce indicated he thought he was working very hard and Mr. Gerund agreed.

Mr. Gerund also individualized student progress which helped avoid the potential frustration Adam might have exhibited during the competitive word game at the end of the period. A phrase was put on the board and the students were given time to make as many words as they could. When it was over, Adam counted his words which were fewer than the other students. Mr. Gerund focused on the amount of word improvement Adam had made compared to past experiences and praised his efforts before moving on to the other students. One way to offset the significant discrepancy among students (while at the same time supporting friendships) would be to have students practice previously learned material in pairs chosen by him. This cooperative learning model can be used during the games he uses also. For instance, if he paired Adam with Tima and Dave with Bruce, the outcomes might be closer than having each student compete against each other.

Lastly, Mr. Gerund used a variety of personal relationship building strategies which show a caring and respect for his students and help him manage their behavior effectively. He was always courteous. "Thank you, sir" and humorous when appropriate, as when a student called out an answer to another student, "that's what I get paid for, do you want me to lose my salary?".

In conclusion, Mr. Gerund exhibited effective teaching during this English lesson. His positive and well-matched expectations, instructional strategies and management tactics contributed to a successful lesson.

Observation of *Phyllis Jones*

Grade 7   **Social Studies**

I visited Mrs. Jones' 7th grade social studies class on Thursday, January 12. This class consisted of a look at how the first Americans used resources for food, shelter and clothing, how archaeologists know they used these resources and the development of an individual chart on important points in a class reading.

Mrs. Jones was concerned about blocks to momentum in her class. She was well provisioned; her materials were out and organized before the start of the class. Student folders were distributed to students as they walked in and on the board was a clear list of what would be needed this period: "Social studies book, folder, white-lined paper, pencil." Students were made aware of this list before instruction began: "The materials you need are on the board." These efforts paid off in that students were ready to participate and were not disruptive seeking materials during instruction.

Both Mrs. Jones and her students knew what was going to happen this period. Her itinerary, given at the beginning of class, was clear (listed above in the second sentence of the first paragraph). Although there were no stated learning objectives for this particular lesson, it was clear that there were several and that the students and teacher were pursuing the same goals—to be able to define certain named terms; describe the job of an archaeologist; describe how the first Americans used natural resources to provide themselves with the necessities of food, shelter and clothing; and take notes while reading a text.

Mrs. Jones checked for understanding using both recall questions ("What are artifacts?" and "Define the term migrate.") and comprehension questions "When looking at and describing the large furry animals on page 82: "What does that say about how man had to hunt? Could they do it alone?" Later, "I wonder how the archaeologists knew about shoes, jackets, coats?"—students came up with the idea that they would get the information from drawings because the original clothing would have disintegrated over time.) She also used the principle of learning called Meaning when the class was discussing the term archaeologist. She and the students used the example of the Harper Middle School being buried and wondered aloud what the archaeologist would find and how he/she would know it was a school. Students keyed in on the task of an archaeologist when discussing what he would find at the school and how he/she might arrive at some conclusions. She used this same technique later in discussing natural resources. First, the students discussed "resources" in relation to Cape Cod (cranberries, seafood), then transferred it to "For ancient man in America, what were his resources?" Thus students' understanding was increased by being able to connect the concept to their own lives. Mrs. Jones also used the blackboard well to highlight important terms and meanings and to demonstrate the setup of a chart to be used during the reading portion of the class.

Mrs. Jones conveys to her students that what they are doing is important and that she is there to assist them. As students were working on their reading chart, Mrs. Jones went from student to student and stopped often to offer advice or assistance. To Michael, who was obviously struggling, she said, "You know what, we're going to have to get together and work on these five. Now, write those three and you and I can work later." In this way, she communicated her confidence that he could do at least some of the problems on his own and the fact that she would be there to help. Her bulletin boards are filled with student work and examples of student thinking, including a food shopping project, travel logs and arrow patterns. Such student work, displayed so appropriately, is a source of motivation and adds to their sense that what they do is important.

Mrs. Jones also makes her expectations clear. For example, when an intrusion was caused by tardy students at the beginning of class (several come from two other homerooms), suggesting that even though this was snack time (6th grade doesn't go to lunch until 1:05), "Those people that come from 102 and 103, please be here by twenty of."

One suggestion about this good class: there needs to be some closure to most lessons, this one included. Mrs. Jones carried an excellent discussion right to the last moment and then said, "Put your papers into your folder—We'll use them later for our writing...May I have the folders?" It would have been helpful to tie together the planned and chance events of the class and, in doing so, she could have checked one more time for understanding.

Observation of *Rose Falcone*

Grade 6   **Writing**

I observed Mrs. Falcone's grade six Project Write class Tuesday, January 31. Mrs. Falcone had the eight students organize their writing folders for the third term and then continue with their writing assignment while she conferenced with individual students about their term and weekly goals.

While the basic concept of this class was good, there were a number of significant problems particularly in the following areas:

1. **Momentum and Routines:** As Mrs. Falcone began her directions for filling out the form that was to be attached to each student's folder, she was interrupted by questions about pencil sharpening, use of the stapler and, a moment later, about staples. These kinds of interruptions could have been prevented by developing and enforcing routines. Allowing these interruptions plus the intrusions of students asking which disk they could use, students wandering and the next class coming into the room before this class ended, served to break whatever momentum there was. In addition, Mrs. Falcone might have smoothed out the confusing first part of this class with more thoughtful provisioning. The folder inserts could have been duplicated after the teacher filled out the various lines (1-Effort 5-Behavior 13-Skills, et cetera) instead of having the students fill them out with oral directions. If that were not possible, then listing the numbers and terms on the board before class would have meant less confusion during the eight minutes it took to accomplish the folder tasks.

2. **Expectations for Student Productivity:** While Mrs. Falcone conducted her one-to-one conferences, she expected the other students to be working productively. "While I'm working with individual students, the rest of you should be working on your compositions in preparation for your response groups." This did not happen. Three young men began putting their latest pieces on the computer, but only one continued this for any length of time. Other students drew pictures, scribbled and/or talked quietly. There was no productive writing done during this class. Students who had finished their piece (e.g. Pat) did not appear to have any other assignment. While Mrs. Falcone seemed aware of some of this non-productive use of time ("Douglas, what do you have down?"), she made no real response to the inactivity that was demonstrated by the blank pieces of paper. Overlapping (managing two or more parallel events simultaneously with evidence of attention to both) is a difficult skill to master, but an important one in a class like this.

Communicating and following through on Expectations is also important.

Mrs. Falcone's individual conferences were well done. She had a list available of important areas of writing which she went over with each of the two students with whom she conferenced in a positive way. "Of these six things, which is your best area? …What is your weakest? (David: "Mechanics.") "I think you are right! Let's set up a goal sheet for you." These interchanges with David and Chris were student-centered, but were structured by the teacher so that both learning and realistic goals would be the outcome. The students' considerable say in the choice of goals gave them a stake in attaining them. The short-term (week) goals were to be attached to the next student paper to serve as an agenda for focused corrections. Her instructions to the students who had already conferenced included a reminder of how these goals might be used: "Make sure you are looking at your goals for the week. If spelling is one, check spelling…." Had this class been a one-to-one tutorial or had she demonstrated the ability to overlap, Mrs. Falcone's approach would have worked well. As it was, her positive efforts with these two students were lost in the non-productivity of the others.

It is suggested that Mrs. Falcone do the following:

1. Establish clear expectations for her students for work habits and work procedures. Pencils should be sharpened before class, students should follow directions (write when told to write) and the next class should wait in the corridor until the present class is dismissed. Mrs. Falcone should make sure that each student knows the in-class assignment and is working *before* she starts one-on-one conferencing activities. Overlapping is much easier to accomplish if students are involved in a productive task as opposed to when they are not on task at all. The end of the period should be a time to check student progress, to assign students to finish work it is not done, and to allow both students and teacher to know what will happen in the next class. This class closure cannot occur if students dismiss themselves as the next group wanders in. Mrs. Falcone's students should have a clear idea of when and how to interrupt for assistance. Only two conferences were held this period, partly because there were so many interruptions.

2. Plan the class carefully, even to the point of visualizing it. If the form students are to work with might be confusing, make up a model and Xerox it; if staples will be needed, have the staples and stapler available. Check the computer paper in the printer before the students need it (both printers malfunctioned this period).

3. Find a way to follow through on instructions. Mrs. Falcone's original

writing directions to the group and individual instructions to David ("Why don't you sit down and throw down some ideas—and then choose one to write on.") were good, but the class didn't write and David didn't jot down ideas. There needs to be some student accountability.

In summary, even though Mrs. Falcone's individual instruction was quite good, her poor class management during this period contributed to what was for most of the class a non-productive forty minutes.

Observation of Freida Smith

Grade 2

The lesson began at 9:00 after all students in the class began working independently in phonics workbooks which had just been given to students for the first time. Mr. Smith called the "Eagles" reading group to the front of the room. With her back turned to the group, she read a summary of the story to herself from the teacher's manual which was resting on a bookcase. It looked as if she was unfamiliar with the story. Mrs. Smith then wrote vocabulary words on the board while referring to the teacher's manual. Much of the ensuing discussion of vocabulary words took place with her back facing the children while she referred to the manual. While she was discussing vocabulary words, some students at seatwork began talking with each other. "How do we do this?" Tommy said aloud. It was apparent that the children were seeking clarification of directions on their phonics workbook exercises. Mrs. Smith reminded these students not to talk by calling out from the small group several times ("I think you have work to do, people," "Someone's disturbing us"). Second graders are rarely self-sufficient with new workbook material. Even if the book itself had not been new, it would be sound practice to go over directions and expectations with students before turning them loose on seat work. This would have avoided student errors, frustration and potential interruption to Mrs. Smith's instructional group.

When finished with the discussion of vocabulary words, Mrs. Smith held up a copy of a basal workbook and read three workbook page directions aloud. Students had not brought their workbooks to the group with them so they couldn't follow the pages. Some of the children watched her as she read, while others looked around the room. It would have been helpful if students could have referred to their own workbook pages for discussion purposes. After some discussion of alphabetization (one workbook page involved this skill), the group was dismissed. However, no directions were given to students about what they should do when they returned to their seats. They returned to their seats and continued working in their phonics workbooks, not the basal workbook whose pages she had just explained.

There was no pre-reading discussion of the story itself with the group. Apparently the students were expected to read it on their own and then do the workbook pages. This approach misses all kinds of opportunities to make meaningful connections with the story, to generate students' interest in it and signals to the students that workbooks are important and literature is not. A second reading group (Bluebirds) was called to the front of the room, and a similar procedure for introducing a story and reviewing workbook directions was used. Mrs. Smith interrupted her presentation at one point, walked out to a child in the seatwork group who had been talking, and placed a three-sided cardboard carrel on his desk. Although no words were exchanged, it was clear that she wanted the child to stop talking. She then walked back to her group and kept looking up at them. She made several comments intended to stop them from talking ("It's getting noisy, people", "I have another set of 'donkey blinders' for someone who needs quiet, so no one can disturb them"). The second group was dismissed, again without reference to what was expected of them when they went back to their seats. The growing noise level among students attempting seatwork seemed obviously connected with their confusion over what was expected. Threatening more 'donkey blinders" not only didn't go over but was an inappropriate response. It smacks of name-calling.

A third group (Hummingbirds) was summoned to the front. During the transition a girl came up to Mrs. Smith and complained that her fingers were beginning to hurt from so much writing in the phonics book. Mrs. Smith told her to take a rest and work on something else; the class had been working now for over forty-five minutes on their new phonics books. This is too long for most second graders and no alternative activities were provided. The girl Mrs. Smith told to "work on something else" needed more specific guidelines; she proceeded to look around the room and to pass notes to her friends. Mrs. Smith asked the Hummingbirds to sit on the floor while they read a new story together. When the story page had been located by several students, one child announced that they read the same story last week. Other students agreed. Mrs. Smith appeared surprised ("Have we??"). She suggested that they read the story aloud anyway. While the students took turns reading aloud, Mrs. Smith interrupted the group twice by reminding the class to quiet down (It's a little bit noisy, people." "People, you have to keep your voices down, you have work to do.")

The number of children talking in the seatwork group increased; the children appeared to be getting tired of writing in their workbooks. She then got up and left her group while individual children were reading aloud and went over to a child in the seatwork group who had been talking. Four more times during the next ten minutes she left the group while a child was reading aloud. The time she did spend with the reading group was very fragmented; when she was sitting with them she stared out at the larger group at least once every 30 seconds. The only comments made to the reading group was how well they were using voice expression ("Good expression," "Your expression could be better"). Mrs. Smith missed many opportunities to check comprehension, stimulate students thinking and make connections around this interesting story of Polar explorers. There was, in fact, no instruction at all delivered during the reading group—only round robin reading.

At ten o'clock, the Eagles (first group) were called back. Mrs. Smith began reading comprehension questions from the teacher's manual directed at the story introduced an hour earlier. The children did not seem to understand. It was then discovered that no child in the group had read the story. Mrs. Smith expressed her amazement when a student explained that he thought they were supposed to be working in their phonics workbooks ""You didn't have to work in the workbooks. You should do reading when I send you back. I'm sorry you didn't understand"). She sent them back to their seat to do the assigned work telling them she would call them back later. At no time when they had been up the first time, however, had Mrs. Smith said to read the story during seatwork. Mrs. Smith needs to be specific in direction-giving when sending students off to work independently.

The Hummingbirds were then called up to discuss the story which had been introduced earlier. The same thing happened as with the first group - no child had read the story. This group was also sent back to their seats. Two more groups met with Mrs. Smith before the lesson ended at 10:30.

In our post observation conference, Mrs. Smith and I discussed the following points. Overall, the lesson was very poorly planned. Mrs. Smith relied heavily upon the teacher's manual for specific guidance. She must become sufficiently familiar with each group's goals and activities in advance in order to give the children a feeling that she is talking to them, rather then to a teacher's manual. The planning for student's independent seat work was not evident at all. Students had been told to work on the first ten pages of the new phonics books; directions for each page were not immediately clear to all students. Much of the initial talking which Mrs. Smith tried to stop was from children seeking to understand specific directions. Most children worked in their phonics workbooks for over an hour and fifteen minutes—a period of time well beyond reasonable attention limits. Since the workbooks did not appear to be coordinated with any specific teaching goal, I felt they were being used as "busy work."

Mrs. Smith must also pay more attention to checking for students learning during the lesson. She appeared more concerned with noise levels than with what students were actually learning. Part of this process should include checking to see that her expectations are being followed through. Such checking would have prevented the situations where two groups returned to discuss a story which the children never read.

Finally, using reading groups as periods of instruction rather than just round-robin reading is a must. I recommended Mrs. Smith try some of the following devices in reading groups:

1. Prior to reading the story have children forecast what they think it will be about based on the title and the pictures.

2. Ask comprehension questions at the end of passage read.

3. Give children questions in advance to read for and have the whole group read a passage silently.

4. After reading a passage, have the child who read it ask a "why" question of another child in the group.

5. Make connections, where possible, between events in the story and children's own experience.

6. Have children practice summarizing in their own words what the main idea of the story was at the conclusion of reading.

The issues of planning, relevance and checking for understanding will be the focus of my next observation. I have asked Mrs. Smith to submit her plan book to me on Monday mornings for the next two weeks to ensure adequate planning in advance of lessons. I am planning weekly observations over the coming months.

APPENDIX C

■

Sample A—Faculty Evaluation Handbook

Faculty Evaluation
H A N D B O O K

TABLE OF CONTENTS

RESOURCES

The Skillful Teacher: Building Your Teaching Skills. Saphier, Jon and Gower, Robert.
Successful Teacher Evaluation. McGreal, Thomas, L. ASCD publication.

Philosophy

The parents, school board members, and staff are committed to having children learn. An effective teacher evaluation system that focuses on the improvement of instruction is critical to student learning.

Evaluation can encourage and facilitate professional growth while assessing performance. It is a cooperative process with the responsibility for accomplishment shared by teacher and evaluator. Ideally, the teacher should be an active participant in all phases of the evaluation process.

Improvement of Learning

The teacher evaluation system stimulates self-evaluation and improvement and creates a continuous focus on improved instruction. The evaluator and staff member share the responsibility for this procedure.

Teacher evaluation is based on five performance expectations:

    I. Classroom Teaching
    II. Contributing Member of Staff
    III. Positive Parent and Community Relationships
    IV. Fulfillment of Routine and Administrative Duties
    V. Continuous Professional Growth and Development

Examples of evidence of teacher performance include classroom observation reports; teacher goals; artifact collection; notes on administrative observation outside the classroom.

Procedures for Improvement of Learning

1. All non-continuing contract staff will be involved in a goal-setting process each year.

2. All continuing contract staff will be involved in a goal-setting process every second year. Participation the first year will be determined by the appropriate evaluator. A continuing contract staff person may participate in the goal-setting process in successive years if deemed necessary or useful by the evaluator or staff member.

3. The goal-setting conference should be held by October 15. (Each year for the non-continuing contract staff member, every other year for the continuing contract staff member.)

4. There are three basic parts to the goal-setting conference:

a. Establishing goals:

Non-continuing contract staff. During the conference the evaluator should take the lead, if necessary, in establishing goals. The recommended guidelines for goal setting as described in Part B should be used.

Continuing contract staff. Continuing contract staff are expected to play an active role in establishing goals. The recommended guidelines for goal setting as described in Part B should be used. If agreement cannot be reached on the goal(s), the evaluator will have final responsibility.

b. Determining methods for collecting data relative to the goals:

As each goal is established, the means for collecting data to determine progress should be determined by the evaluator and the staff member. The three most important recommended methods for collecting data are discussed in Part C.

Non-continuing contract staff. Each non-continuing contract staff member must be involved in the use of all three of the recommended methods. Those staff members not involved in direct instruction would be excused from this requirement.

•*Observation*— each non-continuing contract staff member must be observed in the classroom throughout the year (minimum of three times).

•*Artifact collection*— once during the school year, all artifacts used or produced during the teaching of one unit will be collected and reviewed with the evaluator.

•*Student descriptive data*— at least once during the school year, each non-continuing contract staff member in grades 5-12 will gather information from at least one class of students regarding their perceptions of life and work in the classroom. Each continuing contract staff member in grades 5-12 is encouraged to use a student evaluation form. In all instances student evaluation forms will remain the property of the staff member and will not be used for evaluation data.

Continuing contract staff. The means for collecting data regarding progress should be discussed and agreed upon by the staff member and the evaluator. The methods selected should be appropriate to the goal.

In those instances where agreement cannot be reached, the evaluator has the final responsibility. The evaluator shall make a minimum of two classroom observations with write-ups.

c. A written description of the goal-setting conference:

Attachment A provides a standard form to be used by the evaluator for writing a description of the goal-setting conference. It should be written during or immediately after the conference and shared with the teacher. It should be submitted at the end of the appraisal period as part of the final appraisal write-up.

5. During the actual appraisal period records of the interactions, contacts, and activities between the evaluator and the staff member should be kept. These would include such things as dates and summaries of observations; dates of student evaluations; findings from artifact reviews; and evidence of staff development. It is generally the recording of any and all contacts or data that are appropriate to the methods agreed upon by the evaluator and the staff member during the goal-setting conference.

6. The Summative Evaluation Conference is to be held by the end of the appraisal period (the first week in March for continuing contract staff; by the third week in May for non-continuing contract staff). It is the concluding activity in the appraisal process. Attachment C provides a standard form that should be used for a summary of the conference. The highlight of the conference is the joint discussion of the year's activities, classroom observations, and the implications for future goal setting and continuous self-growth. The summary write up should be done during the conference or immediately afterward. This summative evaluation should be a clear reflection of the discussion during the conference and be shared with the staff member for his or her signature and optional comments.

Every teacher has the right to challenge, in writing, any aspect of his/her evaluation. Such written statements are attached to the evaluation in question and made a permanent part of the teacher's cumulative record. The teacher and evaluator are encouraged to resolve any areas of disagreement.

PART A
CLASSROOM TEACHING

Parameters of Teaching
Listed below are fifteen Parameters of Teaching, taken from the book, *The Skillful Teacher,* which observers will use as guidelines for organizing their feedback to teachers. The Parameters Summary provides further specificity for each of the areas. Each school library has a copy of the text for staff reference.

BASIC QUESTIONS OF THE PARAMETERS OF TEACHING

Parameters	From the Students' Viewpoint	From the Teacher's Viewpoint
Attention	Are students attending to tasks... engaged in the curriculum activity consistently over the period?	Does the teacher have an appropriate range of attention moves and are they working?
Momentum	Are the students free from interruptions, waiting time, distractions and delays?	Does the teacher keep the flow of events moving with smooth, rapid transitions?
Expectations	Do students know exactly what's expected of them? Are the standards appropriate? Do students receive the three key messages: "This is important; You can do it; I won't give up on you"?	Does the teacher communicate expectations clearly? Are the standards high yet attainable? Does the teacher communicate the three messages: "This is important; You can do it; I won't give up on you"?
Personal Relationship Building	Do the students show respect and regard for the teacher?	Does the teacher build good personal relationships with students?
Discipline	Are particularly resistant students dealt with appropriately?	
Principles of Learning	Do students' experiences show opportune use of the principles of learning?	Does the teacher build in productive use of the principles of learning?
Clarity	Are all students understanding the concepts and procedures?	Is the teacher a good explainer? Does the teacher understand the students' understandings and/or misconceptions?
Space	Does the room arrangement support the instruction?	Does the teacher get the most out of the arrangement of space and furniture?
Time	Do students have adequate time to learn? Is the pace appropriate? Are beginning and ending minutes used appropriately?	Does the teacher plan and manage student time investment appropriately?

BASIC QUESTIONS OF THE PARAMETERS OF TEACHING (continued)

Parameters	From the Students' Viewpoint	From the Teacher's Viewpoint
Routines	Do students follow efficient routines for all regularly recurring business?	Does the teacher have the important procedural routines covered and get all the mileage possible out of them?
Models of Teaching	Are the students experiencing an identifiable model of teaching? Is it appropriate?	Can the teacher match different students and learning goals with different models of teaching?
Objectives	Is there a clear and appropriate objective embedded in the instruction?	Has the teacher decided upon a clear objective and framed it properly?
Evaluation	Do students receive systematic evaluation of their work?	Does the teacher know what the students have really learned?
Learning Experiences	Is the learning experience appropriate for students along such items as cognitive level, amount of structure, competition-cooperation, resources used and grouping?	Does the teacher adjust learning experiences for the needs of different students?
Organization of Curriculum	Does the learning experience show continuity, sequence, and integration with other learning experiences the students are having?	Does the teacher plan learning experiences so that they have continuity, sequence, and integration with other learning experiences?

PARAMETERS SUMMARY

CLARITY
Cognitive Empathy
Explanatory Devices
Charts or chalkboard
Analogies
A-V materials
Modeling thinking aloud
Translation into simpler
language
Physical models
Progressive minimal cues
Highlights important info
Mental imagery
Simple cues
Diagrams
Checking
Presses on
Reads cues
"Dipsticks"
Uses recall questions
Uses comprehension questions
Anticipates confusions
Unscrambling Confusions
None
Re-explains
Isolates point of confusion
Returns and perseveres
Has student explain own
current thinking
Speech
Unacceptable
Acceptable
Variety
Matched to group
Matched to individual
Explicitness—not leaving to
implication
Intention of cues
Focus of questions
Necessary steps in directions
Meaning of references
Reasons for activities
The Big Picture
Gives itinerary
Communicates what students
will know or be able to do
Activates students' current
knowledge about concept
Shows resemblance to some-
thing students already know
Makes transitions between
ideas
Foreshadows
Summarizes

ATTENTION
Alerting
Desisting
Enlisting
Acknowledging
Winning

MOMENTUM
Provisioning
Overlapping
Fillers
Intrusions
Lesson Flexibility
Notice
Subdividing
Anticipation

PRINCIPLES OF LEARNING
Application in setting
Meaning
Teach for transfer
Isolate critical attributes
Concrete—semi-abstract—
abstract
Modeling
Similarity of environment
Active participation
Vividness
Feeling tone
End with closure
Breaking complex tasks
Degree of guidance
Close confusers
Say-do
Mnemonics
Sequence & backward chaining
Practice
Contiguity
Cumulative review
Knowledge of results
Reinforcement
Goal setting
Keep students open & thinking

EXPECTATIONS
Communication
Direct
Specific
Repeated
Positive expectancy
Modeled
Tenacious
Prompt feedback on work
Detailed feedback on work
No excuses

Recognition of superior performance
Logical consequences for performance
Communicate 3 Messages:
This is Important
You Can Do It
I Won't Give Up On You
Overall Standards
None
Few consistent
Too low, too high
Average
Inspirational-vague
High but reasonable
Pygmalion Effects

PERSONAL RELATIONSHIP
Ways of Relating:
No way
One way
Variety
Matched
Traits
Fairness
Appearance
Humor
Courtesy
Respect
Realness
Re-establishing contact
Active listening

ROUTINES
Communication
Direct
Specific
Repeated
Consistent
Tenacious
Positive Expectancy
Standards
None
Few consistent
Too low, too high
Average
Inspirational-vague
High/reasonable
Matching
No routines
Few erratic routines
Stable routines
Stable & efficient
Varied routines
Matched to group
Matched to individuals

PARAMETERS SUMMARY

SPACE
Classroom arrangement
No teacher impact
  Conventional
  Varies experimentally
  Uniform & supports instruction
  Varies & supports instruction
  Are ownership & privacy
    provided for?
Are private spaces made available
  for those needing them?
Are the following used?
  Visible, accessible storage
  No dead space
  No teacher blind spots
  Use of vertical space
  Display area
  Active separated from quiet
  Boundaries between areas
  Clear traffic patterns

TIME
Does time allocation per subject
  match teacher & school
  priorities?
Is engaged time 75%+ of time
  allocated to academics?
Does teacher interact with
  students 75%+ of allocated
  academic time?
Do students get adequate time
  w/reteaching if necessary?
Is high success time adequate for
  independent work?
Do students get enough interact-
  ive instruction time with
  teachers?
Are beginning and ending
  minutes used fruitfully?
Scheduling & pacing shows:
  No pattern
  Stable routines
  Variations for teachable
    moments
  Flexibility for changing
    curriculum priorities
  Matching to individual & group

OBJECTIVES
Is there a clear objective that
  creates image of specifically
  what students will know/be able
  to do?

Is the level of difficulty appropriate?
Where do objectives come from?
  Student, Teacher, Group,
    Authority, Contemporary life,
    Culture, Community,
    Disciplines, Needs of Learners,
    Bodies of Information,
    Philosophy
What types of objectives are used?
  Student learning (mastery)
  Generic thinking
  Involvement
  Activity
  Coverage
Is type of objective good fit for
  content?

EVALUATION
Which of these 5 methods is used to
  collect data on student perfor-
  mance?
  Observation
  Work samples
  Tests
  Interviews
  Student self-evaluation
For each method, which of the fol-
  lowing questions can be an-
  swered?
  Is purpose of evaluation clear to
    teacher & students?
  Do tests test what is taught?
  Are criteria for success clear to
    teacher & students?
  Do students get clear & honest
    feedback according to criteria?
  Are there well-organized
    records?
  Are pre- and post-test measures
    taken?
  Is evaluation repeated at future
    date to assess permanence of
    learning?
  Does evaluation provide for
    adequate sample, objectivity,
    accuracy, reliability?
The evaluation is:
  Absent
  Mismatched to content
  Appropriate for content
  Adjusted to group needs
  Adjusted to individual needs

MODELS OF TEACHING
Repertoire of models includes:
  No patterns
  Recitation
  Direct instruction
  A partial model
  A complete model
  A complete model + part.
  Several complete models
Observed models are:
  Inappropriate for students/material
  Appropriate to material
  Matched to group
  Matched to individuals

LEARNING EXPERIENCES
Sources of information
  Convention-constructed
Resources used:
  Text, Teacher, Peers, Parents,
    Interviews, Observation, A-V,
    Reference book, Imagination,
    Experience
Personal relevance
  Contrived, Simulated, Real
Competition
  Competitive, Individual, Coopera-
    tion
Supervision
  Supervised, Facilitated,
    Independent, Matched
Expressing the self
  No, Yes, Matched
Degree of abstraction
  Concrete, Representational,
    Abstract
Cognitive level
  Recall, Comprehension, Analysis,
    Application, Synthesis, Evaluation
Structuring
  No one, Teacher, Student,
    Negotiation (Content, Behavior
    Procedures, Products Closure)
Grouping & interpersonal complexity
  Low, Moderate, High, Match
Information complexity
  Low, Moderate, High, Match
Sensory channels
  Student, input
  Student, motor use
  Student, output
Scale
  Normal, Miniature, Enlarged,
    Matched

PART B
GOAL SETTING

Both the evaluator and the staff member have a responsibility to make the goal-setting conference as productive as possible. The evaluator, while maintaining ultimate responsibility for the final product, must actively involve the staff member in the conference. In most instances, the final goals should be the outgrowth of a cooperative activity. (In working with non-continuing contract staff, the evaluator will normally assume a more directive role in goal setting.) With continuing contract staff, the evaluator's major functions would tend to be as a clarifier and facilitator. When agreement cannot be reached, the evaluator maintains final responsibility. The staff member is responsible for coming to the conference prepared to openly and positively discuss areas that are of particular concern or interest. Both parties share the responsibility of approaching the conference and the entire activity with a positive attitude and a willingness to participate fully.

Number of Goals

The number of goals established between the staff member and the evaluator is less important than the form and substance of the goals. In most cases, the number would range between one and four, with the number being determined by the relevancy and the time and energy required. Goals may be continued from previous years if deemed appropriate.

Goal Priorities

Under normal conditions, it is recommended that goals be established in accordance with their potential impact on student learning. The following priorities should be used as guidelines in determining the appropriateness of goals. However, there are instances when any one of the four types may be relevant and necessary depending on unique conditions.

1. Teacher Goals—Goals built around teacher behaviors or worker behaviors that are directly related to student outcomes. The outline for effective teaching listed in Part A should serve as the basis for setting teaching goals for the regular classroom teachers. Other instructional support personnel should consider direct job-related activities falling under this heading.

2. Learner Goals—Goals that 1) state what a student will know or be able to do; 2) describe a thinking skill or strategy a student will be able to perform; and 3) improve student learning.

3. Program Goals—Goals that relate to curriculum areas, course outlines, articulation activities or materials selection.

4. Organizational or Administrative Goals—Goals that deal with specific administrative criteria such as listed in job descriptions. It is assumed that only in the case of continuing problems in this area would the goal setting procedure be used to help improve the situation.

Measurability of Goals

Part C in the Appendix lists the preferred options for measuring progress towards meeting the goal(s). The key to this activity during the conference is a cooperative effort between the evaluator and the staff member in arriving at a measurable method that fits each goal. Certain goals may be so unique that they force the evaluator and staff person to creatively design a method for assessing progress. This is perfectly acceptable. It is to be remembered that subjective judgments made by the evaluator and the staff person after the method(s) have been applied are clearly acceptable forms of measurement. This allows the teacher and evaluator not to have to confine goals to only those things that are measurable by traditional, empirical standards. For example, if a teacher selected as a goal to build upon student thinking skills, a method for assessing progress might include student hypotheses and/or student inventions.

PART C
TECHNIQUES FOR MONITORING SKILLFUL TEACHING

Several techniques can be employed to collect data about classroom instruction.

Formal Observation

Observing the teacher in the classroom is the most important way of determining teacher effectiveness. Formal observations will be made throughout the school year with either the teacher or evaluator initiating the formal observation process. A post-observation conference will be held following each classroom observation with such conferences being conducted within a reasonable time following the observation—usually not more than seven school days. Information determined in the observation and goal-setting conference will form the basis of discussion in the post-conference.

Artifact Collection

Another way of collecting data is artifact collection. Artifacts might include such things as lesson plans, unit planning materials, tests, quizzes, study guides, worksheets, homework assignments and other materials that affect or relate to instruction. Specific artifacts for assessing the achievement of goals will be those that have been mutually determined to be used for the preparation of the final appraisal report.

Student Evaluation

Great insight can be gained related to instructional effectiveness and effective classroom procedures by asking students for their reactions and perceptions to questions aimed at producing descriptive information about the classroom and the instruction in that classroom. The purpose of any such appraisal is to obtain descriptive data about instruction and not to rate the teacher. Each teacher with classroom responsibilities grades 5-12 is encouraged to have his/her students complete a student evaluation form. All student forms are to remain the property of the teacher. Sample student evaluation forms are available through the principal's office.

PART D
PERFORMANCE EXPECTATIONS IN ADDITION TO CLASSROOM TEACHING

The following are examples of ways in which staff members may choose to fulfill these roles:

I. Contributing member of staff

1. Serves willingly as a committee member

2. Assumes a leadership role among staff members

3. Is involved in whole-school activities

4. Contributes positively to staff meetings

5. Shares special talents, knowledge, and experience with other staff members

6. Serves willingly as mentor to other staff members

7. Participates in sponsoring student activities and events

8. Works cooperatively with all building staff (teacher aides, administration, custodians, lunch program personnel, bus drivers, etc.)

9. Contributes to the accomplishment of district, building, grade level, team, and/or departmental goals

10. Makes curriculum contributions

II. Promotes positive parent and community relationships

1. Communicates effectively at parent conferences

2. Establishes a working relationship with the home

3. Makes special presentations

4. Recognizes and uses community resources

5. Displays sensitivity to the educational needs of students and the expectations of the parents and community

6. Participates on parent boards and committees

III. Fulfillment of routine administrative duties

The extent to which a teacher handles daily tasks efficiently and effectively:

1. Supervises pupils out-of-the-classroom

2. Meets and instructs assigned classes in the locations and at the times designated

3. Maintains accurate, complete, and correct records as required by law, district policy, and administrative regulation

4. Completes assigned reports on time and in a full and accurate manner

5. Performs punctually other assigned non-teaching duties such as bathroom, parking lot, study hall, lunch, homeroom, detention, hallway, etc.

IV. Continuous professional growth and development

1. Participates in professional activities and courses

2. Attends leadership training

3. Introduces classroom innovations

4. Completes significant readings and writings

5. Takes part in study groups

6. Maintains currency in area of expertise

7. Takes part in peer observation

8. Conducts and plans teacher workshops

9. Shows willingness to consider and implement new ideas

ATTACHMENT A

GOAL SETTING REPORT

Staff member _____   Evaluator _____

School _____   Date _____

Goal Setting Conference

A. Establishment and Monitoring of Performance Goals (attach additional material as needed).

Performance Goals for Appraisal Period	**Means for Measuring the Degree to Which the Goal was Reached**

B. Additional Comments Relevant to the Conference.

ATTACHMENT B

OBSERVATION REPORT

Teacher_____ School _____ Grade/Subj. _____

Date_____ Beginning Time_____ Ending Time _____

Observer _____ Announced _____

Unannounced _____

Observations

The observation report will identify teacher's moves and patterns of behavior (claims), supported by quotes or description of behavior (evidence). The report will also include the effect on students or the significance of the teaching act (interpretation) and the evaluator's assessment of the teaching (judgment). Suggestions for growth and/or improvement may also be included. Notes may be attached to the observation form. (For non-teaching positions, this page will be used for a description of performance to date.)

ATTACHMENT B (continued)

Signatures below indicate that a conference between the teacher and the evaluator was held. The teacher's signature on this form indicates that he/she has seen all comments on the form. The teacher's signature does not necessarily indicate agreement with the observation report.

Copy to:

Evaluator _____ Date _____

Teacher _____ Date _____

ATTACHMENT C

SUMMATIVE STAFF EVALUATION

Staff Member _____ School _____ Grade/Subj. _____

Record below in narrative form a description and evaluation of performance in the areas of:

     I.   CLASSROOM TEACHING
     II. CONTRIBUTING MEMBER OF STAFF
     III. PROMOTING POSITIVE PARENT AND COMMUNITY RELATIONSHIPS
     IV. FULFILLING ROUTINE AND ADMINISTRATIVE DUTIES
     V. CONTINUING PROFESSIONAL GROWTH AND DEVELOPMENT
        (use as many sheets as necessary)

ATTACHMENT C (continued)

_____

Recommend unconditional reappointment: Yes [　] No [　]

Recommend reappointment subject to the following conditions: Yes [　] No [　]

_____   _____
Signature of Staff Member   Signature of Evaluator

_____   _____
Date   Date

    Signatures above indicate that a conference between the teacher and the evaluator was held.
The teacher's signature on this form indicates that he/she has seen all comments on the form.
The teacher's signature does not necessarily indicate agreement with the evaluation report.

APPENDIX D

■

Sample B—Faculty Evaluation Handbook

School Administrative Unit #48

TEACHER OBSERVATION AND EVALUATION

TABLE OF CONTENTS

All references are to: Saphier, Jon and R. Gower. *The Skillful Teacher*. Research for Better Teaching, Inc., 56 Bellows Hill Road, Carlisle, MA.
Material has also been drawn from early drafts of Saphier, Jon, *How to Make Supervision and Evaluation Really Work*.

This document is the culmination of over a year of dialogue and study by teacher association representatives and administrators. This is a *DRAFT* that will need adjustments in the future.

In essence the committee recommends that the Saphier model of teacher evaluation be adopted. In addition, the committee recommends that the guidelines for a summative evaluation process be piloted during the 1991-1992 school year.

The Evaluation Committee also wishes to point out that a single administrator should not evaluate more than approximately 12 teachers in a single year if the process is to be of quality. Each observation involves nearly 4 hours [pre-conference (when appropriate), observation, write-up, post-conference]. One teacher, three times a year, plus a summative write-up is approximately 14 hours. That's 168 hours for 12 teachers. We strongly believe that peer observation and coaching can contribute to a resolution of this problem. This recommendation reflects implications that each individual board and association will need to address. Section III of this document proposes a possible approach.

Few educational systems can honestly say they have a well accepted, quality evaluation process. Our teachers and administrators have worked hard to develop a model that can sustain scrutiny and be the cornerstone of a premier school system.

John W. True, Jr.
Assistant Superintendent

PHILOSOPHY

We believe that all children can learn. Therefore, teaching is the most important aspect of our purpose to educate students to the maximum of their potential. We recognize that teachers are learners also and need a collegial and supportive atmosphere in order to thrive. We feel this kind of dynamic and productive environment will result in successful and positive students.

To this end we have developed this document on teacher observation and evaluation.

THE PURPOSE OF TEACHER EVALUATION

We have prepared this guide to assist teachers and administrators in their continuing efforts to improve instruction for our students.

Our values are clear. We believe that teaching and teachers are the heart of the educational process. We believe that teacher performance makes a difference in the achievement of students as well as students' sense of fulfillment and feeling of well-being. We believe that what teachers do and how they do it are important.

Evaluation procedures are provided to:

1. Assist the individual teacher in providing a high quality education for students;

2. Provide a means of periodically assessing individual performance of a teacher over a period of time;

3. Provide information to detail staff members' current performance level, areas of improvement, and suggestions that will lead to further improvement;

4. Identify exceptional educational practices and superior teaching performance.

Even though the emphasis of evaluation is on the concepts listed above, we recognize that teacher evaluation also provides data for personnel practices relating to renewal, promotion, assignment and dismissal.

PRINCIPLES FOR TEACHER EVALUATION

An effective system for teacher evaluation:

1. Ensures that the summative evaluation document contains information that has been reviewed with the teacher as close as possible to the time it happened.

2. Produces a written record of individual activities and growth.

3. Ensures a permanent continuous commitment of the district to the development of its teachers.

4. Makes the experience of teaching more satisfying and more enjoyable.

5. Requires frequent interaction with others in a collaborative setting.

6. Provides activities to study the knowledge base about teaching such as study groups and peer coaching.

7. Provides a structure to have *all* participate in a meaningful way.

8. Includes a systematic way to "enculturate" teachers to be constant learners.

PARAMETERS OF TEACHING

Listed below are fifteen parameters of teaching, taken from the book, *The Skillful Teacher*, which observers will use as guidelines for organizing their feedback to teachers. Each school library has a copy of the text for staff reference and each teacher receives a text after taking the Saphier course.

BASIC QUESTIONS OF THE PARAMETERS OF TEACHING

Parameters	From the Student's Viewpoint	From the Teacher's Viewpoint
Attention	Are students attending to tasks... engaged in the curriculum activity consistently over the period?	Does the teacher have an appropriate range of attention moves and are they working?
Momentum	Are the students free from interruptions, waiting time, distractions and delays?	Does the teacher keep the flow of events moving with smooth, rapid transitions?
Expectations	Do students know exactly what's expected of them? Are the standards appropriate? Do students receive the three key messages? "This is important. You can do it. I won't give up on you."	Does the teacher communicate expectations clearly? Are the standards high yet attainable? Does the teacher communicate the three key messages? "This is important. You can do it. I won't give up on you.?
Personal Relationship Building	Do the students show respect and regard for the teacher?	Does the teacher build good personal relationship with students?
Discipline	Are particularly resistant students dealt with appropriately?	Does the teacher have a repertoire for eliminating disruptions and building cooperation?
Principles of Learning	Do students' experiences show opportune use of the principles of learning?	Does the teacher build in productive use of the principles of learning?
Clarity	Are all students understanding the information and procedures?	Is the teacher a good explainer?
Space	Does the room arrangement support the instruction?	Does the teacher get the most out of the arrangement of space and furniture?

Time	Do students have adequate time to learn? Is the pace appropriate? Are beginning and ending minutes used appropriately?	Does the teacher manage students' time investment appropriately?
Routines	Do students follow efficient routines for all regularly recurring business?	Does the teacher have the important procedural routines covered and get all the benefits possible out of them?
Models of Teaching	Are the students experiencing an identifiable model of teaching? Is it appropriate?	Does the teacher match different students and learning goals with different models of teaching?
Objectives	Are there clear and appropriate objectives embedded in the instruction?	Has the teacher decided upon clear objectives and framed them properly?
Evaluation	Do students receive systematic evaluation of their work?	Does the teacher know what the students have really learned?
Learning Experiences	Is the learning experience appropriate for students relative to items such as cognitive level, amount of structure, competition-cooperation, resources sued and grouping?	Does the teacher adjust learning experiences for the needs of different students?
Organization of Curriculum	Does the learning experience show continuity, sequence and integration with other learning experiences the children are having?	Does the teacher plan learning experiences so that they have continuity, sequence and integration and other learning experiences?

FORMAT FOR OBSERVATION WRITE-UPS

The observation will be written in a narrative format with a structure that uses a series of Claims, Evidence, Interpretation, Judgment and Suggestions.

Claim: a statement that a teacher performs a certain teaching skill or carries out a certain pattern in their instruction (thus, a generalization).

Evidence: a quote or literal description of something said or done.

Interpretation: a statement of what the behavior accomplished or intended to accomplish or what was significant about it—the effect on students.

Judgment: a sentence, phrase, or adjective that lets the reader know what the writer thought of the behavior.

FORMAT FOR SUMMATIVE EVALUATION WRITE-UPS

PERFORMANCE EXPECTATIONS

Teacher evaluation is based on five performance expectations:

I.   Classroom Teacher

II.   Contributing Member of the Staff

III.   Communicator with Parents and Community

IV.   Performer of Routine and Administrative Duties

V.   Constant Learner Responsible for His or Her Own Professional Growth and Development

I. CLASSROOM TEACHER

Reports from *classroom observations* by administrators of teachers are summarized in the Classroom Teaching Section of the summative evaluation form. All formal observations will include a post-conference. Some observations will include a pre- and post-conference between the teacher and administrator, although pre-conferences are not required. What is being observed is the teacher's selection, application and evaluation of the knowledge base on teaching.

This includes the parameters of:

- Clarity
- Momentum
- Objectives
- Discipline
- Time

- Attention
- Expectations
- Routines
- Space
- Learning Experiences

- Principles of Learning
- Models of Teaching
- Student Evaluation
- Personal Relationship Building
- Organization of Learning Experiences

Teachers are expected to continue to add to their repertoire of teaching strategies and increase their capacity to appropriately match these strategies to individual students, groups of students and different curricula.

II. CONTRIBUTING MEMBER OF THE STAFF

Contributing Member of the Staff Section includes such behaviors as how teachers function at department meetings; how they interact with peers on curriculum committees and other task forces; how they reach out to new teachers. There are many ways teachers do things to help colleagues, build team spirit, and further the collaborative goals of the school. This section of the evaluation report is where an evaluator summarizes feedback on how well the teacher works with other professionals. Including this role in teacher evaluation signals that we expect teachers to play a positive role in the organization outside their classrooms

III. COMMUNICATOR WITH PARENTS AND COMMUNITY

How well teachers communicate with parents and the broader community is another important role of the job. One can observe such performance at Back-to-School night, during parent conferences, and at the numerous points of contact between teachers and parent and community members. This section of the evaluation write-up is the place to note any projects or ways in which a teacher has extended him or herself to give information to parents or build bridges between the school and the community. It is also the place to note any obstacles the teacher may be posing to good communication.

IV. PERFORMER OF ROUTINE ADMINISTRATIVE DUTIES AND OBLIGATIONS

Teachers are also expected to do routine administrative functions such as hall duty, cafeteria duty, taking attendance, and filling out reports and ordering new materials. It is legitimate to comment on how well they carry out these responsibilities.

V. CONSTANT LEARNER RESPONSIBLE FOR HIS OR HER OWN PRO-FESSIONAL DEVELOPMENT
The fifth section for comment, "Own professional development," signals that we expect teachers to be constant learners, and we want to credit them for the efforts they make toward their own professional growth. By the same token, we need to be able to use evaluation to deal with a teacher who gets in a rut and will do nothing to stretch and learn.

This section is done by the teacher.

Other than section I, the other four sections may, in fact, contain only a few sentences each. The exception would be, for example, the case of a teacher who has done something significant with community members that helped the school. Thus, for this person, section III of the report would be longer than a few sentences. Another example would be a teacher who has less than satisfactory relations with other staff members to the degree that it is impeding the successful functioning of the staff. In this case, section II of the report would be longer and contain claims, evidence, interpretation, judgments and suggestions just like a classroom observation report.

ANY NEGATIVE DOCUMENTATION FOUND IN THE SUMMATIVE EVALUATION MUST BE DOCUMENTED AS CLOSE TO THE TIME OF THE OCCURRENCE AS POSSIBLE.

MAKING EVALUATION WORK

The following five tenants must be present for this evaluation system to work:

1. COMMON LANGUAGE AND CONCEPT SYSTEM
   The foundation of all desirable outcomes for observations is having a *common language and concept system for talking about teaching* so professionals can communicate meaningfully about what is going on in classrooms.

   All true professionals have a professional vocabulary that draws on a disciplined body of knowledge.

   Creating a background document of "Criteria for Effective Teaching" creates an important opportunity for us to really state our values about teaching and learning.

   The language used in the book, *The Skillful Teacher*, and in courses, "Understanding Teaching I and II" and "Observing and Analyzing Teaching I and II" is the language we will use.

2. EVALUATE THE EVALUATORS
   To make supervision and evaluation really work is a commitment to improving the process. The significant decision-makers of a district, including school board and superintendent, must show by word and deed that their commitment is real. It means using the goal-setting process annually to reiterate the goal; it means committing time, money, and training resources to the goal of effective teaching and in the case of evaluation, it means formally evaluating the evaluators on their ability to evaluate.

3. TRAINING FOR ADMINISTRATORS AND TEACHERS
   Few administrators have systematic training in classroom observation when selected for the job and few ever get it later. Ample materials are available for this kind of training. The starting point is the knowledge base on teaching. Administrators need to learn with academic rigor the concepts from the knowledge base and then practice looking for, noticing and recording in good notes occurrences of important teaching behaviors. They need to know how to analyze their notes and produce observation reports which have a balance of claims, evidence, interpretation, judgment and suggestions. They also have to be able to write summative evaluation reports which include judgments, supported by evidence.

   Teachers need training in the knowledge base on teaching and how to do peer observation and problem solving with colleagues. Some of them may receive additional training as study group leaders as a way to infuse the study of teaching into the ongoing life of the school.

4. SYSTEMATIC INDUCTION AND TRAINING OF NEW PERSONNEL (BOTH ADMINISTRATORS AND TEACHERS)

This is an obvious recommendation, but one that is often ignored after a system completes the initial training process for the people presently in the system. Unless someone plans for how new administrators and teachers are inducted into the culture of the system, it will not happen. This recommendation carries with it the implication that ongoing professional development for administrators is a district mission along with ongoing professional development opportunities for teachers.

Teaching and learning and what goes on between teachers and students day to day, class to class, is the center of our business. It is the most important part of our business. Our induction procedures for new personnel, both teachers and administrators, should signal this value if we believe it.

5. AT-RISK AND DISMISSAL PROCEDURES AND PRACTICES

These procedures pertain to a very small number of people. They must be (and be seen as) prompt, fair, humane, and courageous...

Prompt in that teaching problems are not allowed to slide since children are losing daily when teachers are doing a poor job;

Fair in that teachers subject to these procedures have every chance to improve and significant genuine energy goes into helping them to do so;

Humane in that teacher' feelings are recognized and support is offered. Sometimes job counseling and professional time for job hunting will be given.

Courageous in that administrators really write observation reports that provide evidence of inadequate teaching and give suggestions and help for improvement.

ALTERNATIVE EVALUATION PROPOSAL
FOR YEAR TWO OF A
TWO-YEAR EVALUATION CYCLE

Staff members on continuing contract whose evaluations have been satisfactory may choose to submit an Alternative Evaluation Proposal or continue formal evaluation. The alternatives to evaluation should be designed to encourage and enable teachers to reflect upon their teaching. Their proposal would include the following information:

- the *General Category* of the proposal,
- the *Goals* of the proposal,
- the *Actions* or *Procedures* they will follow to accomplish the goal,
- what *Evidence* they will provide that shows the accomplishment of the goal,
- other *Teacher Participants* and if so, their roles and responsibilities, and
- what type of *Support* is needed from the administrator.

1. PEER OBSERVATION
    Teachers agree to observe each other's classes 3-4 times during the year and provide and receive feedback important to their goal.

2. STUDY GROUPS
    Teachers meet with colleagues in groups of 4-8 to learn new strategies, experiment with these strategies and share the results of their experiments, and to problem solve. Study groups can be developed to feature content which would support a teacher's goal.

3. FIELD BASED RESEARCH
    In this category, a teacher develops a hypothesis and a research project to test that hypothesis. A teacher might propose the hypothesis that the use of cooperative learning strategies will improve student achievement in U.S. History. The teacher could then identify a section or sections in which to use the strategy and measure student achievement. Findings could be briefly presented in a paper and discussed with other teachers.

4. ANALYSIS OF A PORTFOLIO OF ARTIFACTS
    A teacher could maintain a file which includes each lesson plan, hand-out, quiz, test and exam in a given semester. The analysis might include the congruency between what is taught and what and how it is tested; the relationship between the instructional strategies used and student achievement.

5. WEEKLY JOURNAL
A teacher could reflect upon what worked and what didn't work in their teaching and record their thoughts each week in a journal which could be shared with other teachers or their administrator. Or the teacher could use the journal as a basis for self-evaluation of his/her goal.

6. PREPARING AND PRESENTING A STAFF DEVELOPMENT PROGRAM
A teacher with interest and expertise in a particular area of instruction could develop and present a program on the topic to other interested staff. The presentation should include what participants will know or be able to do as a result of participating in the program, why it is important to learn it and how it relates to student learning.

7. TEAM TEACHING WITH AN ADMINISTRATOR OR PRINCIPAL
A teacher could plan, teach and evaluate a unit with an administrator or principal (two to three weeks). Both would share the responsibility for developing, presenting and assessing the unit and identifying its problems and successes.

8. SUBMISSION OF ARTICLES FOR PUBLICATION
A teacher could prepare and present two or three articles on instruction and/or curriculum for publication in professional journals.

9. SELF-ANALYSIS OF VIDEOTAPES
A teacher could videotape three different lessons during the course of the year, analyze the lessons and write up an assessment on the effectiveness of each.

10. EXTENDED MENTORING
A teacher could develop and/or extend mentoring relationships throughout the school. The mentoring process should include observing the new teacher at several points throughout the year, providing feedback, being observed by the teacher and holding frequent discussions about teaching.

11. OTHER (if considered appropriate by the administrator)

ALTERNATIVE EVALUATION PROPOSAL

NAME _____

SCHOOL _____ Date _____

1. State the General Category of the proposal (see attached suggestions).

2. State the Goals of your proposal.

3. State the Actions or Procedures you will follow to accomplish this goals.

4. What Evidence will you provide that shows completion of your proposal?

5. Will there be other Teacher Participants involved in this proposal? If so, name them and give their role and responsibility.

6. What, if any, type of support (materials, time, staff development meetings) would you like from your administrator which are necessary to the completion of your project?

Teacher's Signature _____ Date _____
Evaluator's Signature _____

OBSERVATION REPORT

TEACHER_____   SCHOOL _____

GRADE/SUBJECT _____   DATE _____

OBSERVER _____ Announced ____ Unannounced _____
(Check one)

BEGINNING TIME _____ ENDING TIME _____

The observation report will identify the teacher's moves and patterns of behavior (**CLAIMS**) supported by quotes or descriptions of behavior (**EVIDENCE**). The report will also include the effect on students or the significance of the teaching act (**INTERPRETATION**) and the evaluator's assessment of the teaching (**JUDGMENT**). **SUGGESTIONS** or **RECOMMENDATIONS** for growth and/or improvement may also be included.

Evaluator _____ Date _____

Teacher _____ Date _____
    The teacher's signature on ;this form indicates that s/he has seen all comments on the form. The teacher's signature does not necessarily indicate agreement with the evaluation report.

Copy to Superintendent's office for review and file

Part 2 of 2

SUMMATIVE STAFF EVALUATION

Staff Member _____

School _____ Grade/Subject _____

Record below in narrative form a description and evaluation of performance in the areas of:

    I.   Classroom Teaching (Claims from observation reports)

    II.   Contributing Member of the Staff

    III.   Communicator with Parents and Community

    IV.   Performer of Routine Administrative Duties and Obligations

    V.   Constant Learner Responsible for His or Her own Professional Development (done by teachers)

(Use as many sheets as necessary.)

(THE SUMMATIVE EVALUATION SHOULD CONTAIN "NO SUPRISES".)

I recommend to the Superintendent for
renewal of the teacher's contract.   _____

I recommend to the Superintendent for renewal of the teacher's
contract with reservations subject to the following performance
standards and conditions. (see attached)   _____

I do not recommend to the Superintendent for the
renewal of the teacher's contract.   _____

_____   _____
        Signature of Staff Member   Signature of Evaluator

_____   _____
                    Date   Date

The teacher's signature on this form indicates that s/he has seen all comments on the form. The teacher's signature
does not necessarily indicate agreement with the evaluation report.

Copy to the Superintendent's office for review and file.

Attachment A

The teacher is recommended for renewal of contract with reservations subject to the following performance standards and conditions:

Evaluator's Signature _____   Teacher's Signature _____

Attachment B

The following is a brief review of why the teacher is not recommended for renewal

(Attachment B applies to non-probationary teachers only)

Evaluator's Signature_____   Teacher's Signature _____

OUTLINE OF REPRIMAND STEPS

- VERBAL DISCUSSION

- VERBAL DISCUSSION AND MEMO IN FILE

- VERBAL DISCUSSION AND LETTER IN FILE

- VERBAL DISCUSSION, LETTER AND SOME KIND OF FORMAL ACTION

Steps may not follow sequence depending on seriousness of incident or issue.

APPENDIX E

■

Sample
Final Evaluation Summary Report

FINAL EVALUATION SUMMARY — Jane Renaldi

I. Classroom Teaching

I observed Jane teach French on three different occasions this year. Jane's goals for the year included oral fluency as well as knowledge of grammar and skill in reading and writing French. Because the classes observed range from French 3 to French 5, the objectives and activities were different.

"Magical" is the word that best describes Jane's teaching, but a close examination reveals that the magical effects (students eagerly responding to questions, speaking French to each other as well as to the teacher, and bringing their own ingenuity to skits in French) are the result of skill and craft in the various parameters of teaching. For example, she is clear in presenting new information, and she systematically checks to see whether students have understood. She uses a variety of explanatory devices including physical models (The Pepsi can or the Carefree gum in the "magic box" she uses to introduce new vocabulary words); the chalkboard (she has students write answers to homework on the board and corrections are made together); and gestures (She gestures toward the back with her eyes and hands to suggest the "past." She adjusts speech to match the situation and checks for understanding by reading nonverbal clues and by probing with follow-up questions.

The work behind the "magic" is certainly apparent in the way Jane incorporates the principles of learning into her teaching. As should be expected of a foreign language teacher, she makes effective use of the more technical principles of learning, those which apply most directly to the learning of discrete bits of information (new vocabulary words) or specific operations (making the adjective agree with the noun it modifies.) But Jane's purpose is to go beyond the mastery of sufficient vocabulary and grammar in order to enable students to become comfortably fluent speakers, readers, and writers of French. She creates settings in which students can practice speaking not just French sentences in strict practice format, but in skits and role plays where she may be the technical adviser, lighting technician, camera person, and director. In fact, because her teaching is designed to help students transfer their French knowledge and skills, she creates a variety of opportunities for speaking in class (the televised skits, the conversational discussions about movies, the humorous conversations about the quality of French and Spanish champagnes.) She has created a feeling tone in the class which is most productive for learning. There is fun, but also seriousness about work. The students compete to demonstrate their knowledge of vocabulary words, and they want everything to be perfect, right down to every accent mark on their script.

Jane has a wide variety of attention moves she uses when needed: mild desists, naming, winning with humor are threaded together effectively. The pace of the instruction and the variety of the activities keeps kids involved so there are no breaks in momentum. Every minute is used for instruction. One episode we discussed after the second observation (11/9) was the benefit of being more explicit ahead of time in telling students what to look for and why in viewing films.

Jane has high expectations for her students. To reinforce her objective of oral fluency, she reminds students that there will be no speaking in English, only French. She states her expectations directly and enforces them in formal situations (reviewing homework) and in a variety of less formal classroom situations before and after class. She expects all her students to live up to her expectations in using the language and in participating in class. She conveys positive expectations for students meeting her standards and enforces them sensitively yet persistently.

Students try hard to meet her expectations because she has established a strong personal relationship with them. Her sense of humor enables her to help students see French as a medium for communicating humor as well as grammatical constructions (the Charles DeGaulle box, the skit, the "Bravos" to congratulate winners in the magic box game.) She conveys a sense of realness by responding openly and sharing her own experiences. Her own energy and enthusiasm are contagious.

Jane uses a "magic box" and uses the "magic of television" but the real magic comes from combining her enthusiasm and energy with strong teaching skills. She knows where she's headed, and she succeeds because she is strong in virtually all the parameters of teaching, and she has learned to integrate the moves from many different parameters in the service of clearly defined objectives. Bravo!

II. Contributing Member of Staff

Jane is a well-respected member of the staff. She attends house and staff meetings, and when she does choose to speak up, she always has something worthwhile to contribute. She has good working relationships with counsellors and teachers, in fact, she used her position as a teacher to help students connect with various support networks (department, house, etc.) in the school.

III. Community and Parent Relationships

I have received only positive feedback about Jane from parents who praise her teaching. She has worked closely with the French teacher at _____ Junior High School and has visited the school to talk to eighth graders about taking French in the high school.

IV. Routine and Administrative Duties

Jane has a homeroom, a duty which she fulfills reliably and cheerfully.

V. Continuing Professional Growth and Development

This has been an important year for Jane in terms of her own professional growth and development. She has taken two courses, one in public speaking and one in the essentials of writing. Both courses have been particularly helpful in creating new classroom activities and in developing her own skills in preparation for consulting with other teachers. By sharing her work on oral fluency with others in the department, she has also influenced the development of others' teaching.

In addition to attending seminars and conferences of professional organizations, (e.g., Mass. Foreign Language conference), Jane will be giving a presentation on using video to teach French at the MFLA conference in May. She is now designing a curriculum package, including video tapes, a workbook, and a teacher's manual. The process of drafting a few chapters and of meeting with her publisher for editing has provided her with valuable feedback which she plows back into her teaching and her curriculum writing. She is also pursuing the Proficiency testing license awarded by ACTFL; she has attended the Boston University program and expects to finish this summer.

APPENDIX F

Key Steps in Developing a Good
Supervision/Evaluation System

KEY STEPS IN DEVELOPING
A GOOD SUPERVISION/EVALUATION SYSTEM

1. Joint agreement (teachers, administrators, parents) on criteria for effective teaching (general areas, not a checklist).

2. School system commitment to improving supervision/evaluation as a multiple-year goal.

3. Superintendent supervises and evaluates administrators regularly (monthly) around developing skills in supervision/evaluation.

4. Skill training, multi-year, for all administrators, including:

   - common language and concept system for talking about teaching
   - analyzing teaching using claims and evidence
   - writing clearly
   - conferring skills
   - dealing with tough conferences
   - case reviews, personal coaching
   - time management
   - delegating and prioritizing.

5. Including teachers in skill training around observing and analyzing teaching.

6. Expectation that evaluations comment on all 5 important roles of a teacher.

7. Observations and evaluations that are narrative...no points or grades.

8. Principals willing to take stands; courage with support and encouragement.

9. Holding department chairs accountable for honest evaluations.

10. Requiring new supervisors and new teachers to study the knowledge base on teaching and become enculturated into the common language and concept system.

11. Increasing the frequency of observation, feedback, and substantive discussion with and between teachers to minimum of 6x/yr+.

12. Making the personnel and structural changes necessary to accomplish increased frequency of observation of teaching.

APPENDIX G

■

Criteria for a Good Teacher Evaluation System

CRITERIA FOR A GOOD TEACHER EVALUATION SYSTEM

1. It provides frequent, systematic, informed analysis and feedback to teachers on their teaching. Purpose? Cheerleading, validation of effective practices, stimulation for further growth and improvement, expansion of repertoires, stretching teaching thinking.

2. It embodies a clear position about what the district thinks is most important in a teacher's performance, that is, what the district values and expects a person to do in teachers' multiple roles.

3. It provides a fair and thorough way to document incompetent or unsatisfactory teaching and dismiss people who can't meet district standards.

4. It provides a clear way of identifying teachers whose performance is less than satisfactory that a) makes it clear to all other staff that they are *not* at risk and b) provides genuine help and adequate resources for the teacher at risk to improve.

5. Those who evaluate are trained and continue professional development in the skills of observing acutely, comprehensively and writing clearly with a balance of claims, evidence, interpretations, and judgments.

6. Those who evaluate are evaluated on their ability to evaluate!

7. Evaluation that "counts" is insulated from supervision for improvement by separate procedures and calendar periods (though not necessarily by different personnel.)

CRITERIA FOR A GOOD OBSERVATION FORM

1. It has a background document that defines important areas of teaching performance.

2. It allows people to say narratively what they have to say; that is, it is blank, non-categorical, with no lines or boxes.

3. It makes no grades or comparative ratings of teachers.

CRITERIA FOR A GOOD FINAL EVALUATION FORM

1. It requires comment in narrative form on each major role of a teacher (classroom instructor, member of staff, routine duties, communication with parents and community, efforts for one's own professional development).

2. (Same as 2 above)

3. (Same as 3 above) except in the case of a teacher whose overall performance is less than satisfactory by district standards, in which case such is specifically designated.

APPENDIX H

■

Bibliography
Key Studies of School Culture

KEY STUDIES ON SCHOOL CULTURE

Goodlad, John. *A Place Called School: Prospects for the Future*. New York: McGraw-Hill, 1984.

Hopkins, David. "Integrating Staff Development and School Improvement: A Study of Teacher Personality and School Climate." Bruce Joyce Ed., *Changing School Culture Through Staff Development*. Alexandria, Va.: A.S.C.D., 1990.

Little, J.W. "Norms of Collegiality and Experimentation: Workplace Conditions of School Success." *American Educational Research Journal,* Fall 1982.

Mortimore, P., P. Sammons, L. Stoll, D. Lewis, R. Ecob. *School Matters: The Junior Years*. London: Open Books, 1988.

Purkey, Stewart C. and Marshall S. Smith. "Effective Schools: A Review." *The Elementary School Journal*, March 1983.

Rosenholtz, Susan. *Teachers' Workplace: The Social Organization of Schools*. New York: Longman, 1989.

Rutter, Michael et al. *Fifteen Thousand Hours: Secondary Schools and Their Effects on Children*. Cambridge: Harvard University Press, 1979.

Saphier, J.D. and M. King. "Good Seeds Grow in Strong Cultures." *Educational Leadership*, March, 1985.

APPENDIX I

■

Pre and Post-Conference Guidelines

COMPONENTS OF PRE-OBSERVATION CONFERENCES

Before the Lesson
....teacher and observer discuss/clarify (in any sequence):

1. What is *mastery or thinking objective of the lesson?*

2. What has *led up to/will follow this lesson?*

3. What is the *sequence of events* within the lesson/experiment?

4. What teaching strategies/behaviors will the teacher be *experimenting* with?

5. What *student behaviors* does the teacher hope to hear/see?

6. How are the teaching strategies, desired student behaviors and desired outcomes/objectives *related?*

7. Does the teacher have *any particular concerns* regarding any of the above? Or *any additional information* she/he would like to share with observer?

8. What *kind of data* would the teacher like the observer to collect during the observation?

9. *In what form* should the observer collect the data?

During the lesson...

Observer *records literally* whatever data was agreed upon in the pre-conference.

adapted from Costa and Garmston
"Cognitive Coaching" training

QUESTIONS FOR POST-OBSERVATION CONFERENCES

After the lesson
...the teacher reflects...the observer follows the lead of the teacher

1. How did you (the *teacher*) *feel* about the lesson or the experiment?

2. What do you *remember* about the *students' behaviors*? How did the students' behavior *compare* to what you had planned/hoped for?

3. How did your own *teaching strategies and behaviors compare to what you had planned/hoped for?*

4. To what extent were your *objectives* achieved?

5. *Why* do you suppose this lesson worked? Didn't work?

6. What *insights or conclusions* do you draw from this lesson?

7. If you were to do it again, is there any way in which you'd *re-shape* it? What are "*keepers*"?

8. What are you finding *useful/helpful about this observation process?* Is there anything we might want to do differently next time?

As it is relevant
or when the teacher asks for it,
the observer
shares data and asks related questions.

COMBINING DATA AND QUESTIONS
RATHER THAN JUDGING

The general pattern here is to give data, then, if appropriate, ask for the person's feelings, interpretation or rationale.

"What were you thinking...How did you feel about it when..."

Examples of questions by observers that stimulate reflection from a teacher:

1. Questions that clarify observed actions, events or statements...
   "I couldn't see very well; what was John doing when you told him to 'cut it out!'?"

2. Questions that clarify tone or feelings associated with a particular situation...
   "I noticed that you started talking much more quickly when you described what you wanted students to be concentrating on in their groups. What were you feeling at that point?"

3. Questions that clarify the reasons and intended consequences of observed actions, events or statements...
   "I noticed you stopped John in the middle of his answer and went to Peggy. What were you thinking when you did that?"

4. Questions that ask about the reasons for repeated patterns or incidents of the same nature...
   "I noticed that each time you went back to the circle you always knelt down in the same spot. Was there a particular reason for that?"

5. Questions that connect an observation with a past conversation or event.
   "Was that the kind of reaction you were telling me about when we were discussing John?"

   "Was Susie one of the kids whom you thought might not participate?...And she talked 4 times. What do you think was going on for her?"

APPENDIX J

■

Artifacts from Creation of a
Four-Year Professional Growth Cycle
in a New York District

LETTER TO ALL STAFF, CO-SIGNED BY SUPERINTENDENT AND TEACHERS' UNION PRESIDENT

Dear Colleagues,

All plans for supervision and evaluation aim at continuous improvement of instruction. We want ours to as well. But in addition we would like to come up with a professional growth plan that achieves more.

The state of New York has required that a written statement of performance be done each year on every teacher. Therefore it is necessary to reexamine what we do in each year of the current four year evaluation cycle. We would like this reexamination to produce a plan with broad-based support throughout the district and use it as an opportunity to move ahead rather than just meet a state regulation. Move ahead toward what? ...toward a professional growth cycle that would achieve the following outcomes:

Professional Growth Cycle

1. *Every year* teachers have a chance for substantive, helpful conversations about their teaching with someone who is knowledgeable about what they do and can help them reflect on their decision-making with students. (Teaching is too isolated and lonely a profession.)
2. The school as a workplace becomes a more satisfying, growth-oriented environment for adults. (The better the working environment for adults, the better the learning for students.) Thus the plan must manifest our commitment to the development of people at all stages of their careers.
3. The district has a clear and fair set of procedures for dealing with teachers whose performance is less than satisfactory, a set of procedures which is clearly signalled when it kicks in and is clearly different from standard practices for everyone else.
4. Administrators play a more significant role in teachers' staff development. To do this they need to continue gaining skills as observers and analysts of instruction so they can be better staff developers.
5. Teachers play a more significant role as staff developers of each other.

Therefore we are forming a joint committee of teachers and administrator to examine what we do each year of the four-year cycle. We are asking them to come up with a plan that will meet the state law in such a way as to accomplish the five outcomes above. We already do evaluation; this is a chance to create a "Professional Growth Cycle" that will do more.

Signed by the Superintendent and Teachers' Union President

PROPOSAL OF PRINCIPLES FOR
PROPOSED GROWTH CYCLE

The plan for a multi-year professional development cycle.

1. Should make the experience of teaching more satisfying and more fun.
2. Should provide for choices, alternatives and decision making by teachers about what they do.
3. Should require interaction with others frequently in a collaborative setting at least once every other year in the cycle and encourage people to work with others outside their grade level/department and sometimes their building.
4. Should have as an important component a common language and conceptual system about effective teaching.
5. Should have activities available to study the knowledge base about teaching each year at the building level, such as a study group on clarity or a workshop on questioning techniques.
6. Should be simple and easy to manage, free from cumbersome paperwork and procedures.
7. Should be taken seriously by all and all are expected to participate in a meaningful way.
8. Should be thought of as a permanent, continuous commitment of the district to the development of its people.
9. Should itself be evaluated periodically and be open to revision.
10. Should produce a written record of individual activities and growth at the end of each year.
11. Should involve teachers in the management and governance of the structures that come out of this plan for a multi-year cycle.
12. Should encourage experimentation in one's teaching.
13. Should have adequate resources to make it work.
14. Should clearly separate administrative evaluation for job decisions from the rest of the cycle.
15. Should include a systematic way to enculturate new teachers to being constant learners, help them learn the operation and procedures of the school and how to receive help from colleagues.
16. Should, *apart from administrative observations and evaluations, require people to receive frequent (6-8 times per year) observational feedback at least once during the cycle* about something specific in their teaching from someone knowledgeable about the thing being observed.
17. Should provide some evidence of continuity, development and growth over the years in what the district offers and what people do for their personal growth. (Implies long-range personal goal setting and planning.)
18. Should provide for people at different levels of professional maturity from apprentice to senior teacher.
19. Should build in ways for teachers to get recognition and support for their growth, their improvements and their achievements.

SUMMARY OF PROFESSIONAL GROWTH CYCLE
COMMITTEE MEETING
ON MAY 14th AT MIDDLE SCHOOL

Jon started the meeting with a few propositions:

1. "Closing the loop" will be very important in our process...that is, getting back to people in ones, twos, small groups, to show how their input was considered in this committee's process.

2. Discussions should provoke different points of view, debate, open discussion and lots of it.

We started the meeting with a discussion of input and reaction from each school's faculty. From this discussion we developed the following eight questions to consider.

1. How can we make the four-year cycle more flexible?

2. Who will approve teachers' plans for professional development each year?

3. Who will monitor the plans and how?

4. What is a "pilot"?

5. What resources will we need to carry out the cycle?

6. How will we keep records on which teachers do what?

7. How frequent will observations be in the observation year?

8. How do these activities in the different years fit in with the state's evaluation requirement?

We answered these questions as follows:

1. **Flexibility:** teachers can decide each year whether they wish to do the observation, collaborative or individual year of the cycle, as long as each one occurs once during the three years. Once every four years, however, teachers will systematically rotate through the evaluation year as determined by the principal. So in which of the four years evaluation will occur is not a choice; which of the remaining three years in the cycle is observation, collaborative or individual *is* a teacher choice.

    Determining if there is a need for a system to decide who and how many people do what year of the cycle will be a building level decision. (There was some sentiment that a uniform bottom line for each building might be to shoot for about a quarter of the staff in each category each year, but that was left open.)

2. **Who approves teachers' plans?** We decided that all plans are automatically approved. However, each building will have a

review committee consisting entirely of teachers, including the building representative currently on this four-year cycle committee. This committee will review plans submitted by teachers to make sure each plan meets the criteria for the year it aims at: that is, does this plan for the collaborative year meet the criteria for the collaborative year; does this plan for the observation year meet the criteria for the observation year; does this plan for the individual year meet the criteria for the individual year?

To do this job, these committees, as well as all the teachers in the district, need a clear definition of what these criteria are. Rick will bring three draft definitions to our next meeting on May 29 for review by the four-year cycle committee.

The teacher committee in each school will consist of five teachers, three of whom will be a quorum. It is not expected that this committee will have to meet very much. However, this is one of the questions that will be answered during the pilot year.

At the end of each plan, teachers are requested to answer two questions in a check box. Question A: Would you like feedback on your proposal? Question B: Would you like help in organizing resources to carry it out? If a large number of people want feedback and help, the local building committee will have to spend more time doing its job.

If the local building committee comes across a proposal that does *not* meet the criteria, it is the responsibility of the committee to contact the teacher and discuss this with him/her. However, the main purpose of the local building committee is to hear, validate, offer suggestions if wanted, and signify as important the fact that people are taking the time to write proposals and to plan their professional development. Once the cycle is working, teachers will be expected to submit their proposals to the building committee by September 30. This, however, will not be enforced next year as we are not sure what our time line will be yet.

Copies of teachers' proposals also go to the principal, not for approval, but so the principal has a document to file as part of meeting the state evaluation requirement.

3. **Who monitors teachers' plans and how?** At the end of the year teachers will submit a record of their activities and a summary statement of what they learned or got out of the experience. This document will be two sides maximum. The building level committee will review all of the records teachers submit to see overall if the process of the four-year cycle is working. In

addition, they will take the responsibility to speak to individual faculty members who did not submit a record or who did not carry out their proposals.

Further, we have agreed that the representatives on the four-year cycle committee should bring up the monitoring issue with each faculty: "What should we do in the case of people not carrying out their proposals?" We are not expecting that to happen, but if it does we have to be prepared to deal with it and we have to raise with our faculties the issue of *how*, as a professional staff, we should deal with it.

Copies of teachers' completed records also go to the principal for inclusion in the file and satisfaction of the state evaluation requirement.

4. **What is a pilot?** In this case the pilot year of the four-year cycle has as its purpose the generation of ideas to change and improve the four-year cycle. The purpose of the pilot is not to decide whether or not we will do a four-year cycle. The purpose is to decide how to accomplish the objectives of the four-year cycle as outlined in the philosophy document and how to work the bugs out of the system that we first will try.

This brought us to a discussion of how much, how fast, starting when? There was some discussion as to whether or not the four-year cycle should be piloted at all during the '87-88 school year. Resolving this will be one of the most important questions at the May 29 meeting.

If we *did* start next year, the following time line was proposed:

   a) During May and June reports to the faculty on where we have gotten so far with our planning and what questions are still open.

   b) September would be used to continue discussions of these open questions with faculties, particularly issues around what should happen if people do not carry out their proposals and other issues summarized above.

   c) Teachers would be expected to hand in their proposals by October 30, by which time the building committee would have been chosen and the pilot year would then commence.

We are still undecided, however, about whether the starting date of October 30 should be pushed later in the year, or whether the whole '87-88 should be a planning year with the actual pilot to begin '88-89. We are agreed, however, that when we start we should start for everybody all at once with all aspects of the plan.

5. **Resources:** We did not finish this issue but covered the following points:

   a) Ballpark figure: approximately 30 sub days per building would be required to cover the collaborative/observational proposals.

   b) Training should be planned for teachers on notetaking when they are observing each other.

   c) In-service activities should be in place to provide workshops on things teachers might want to practice and observe each other for.

   Discussing what resources are necessary to carry out the four year cycle is one of the big issues to discuss with building faculties next fall.

6. **Records:** This has been handled in number 2 and 3 above.

7. **Frequency of Observation:** The consensus is to recommend a minimum of four.

8. **Relation of these activities to the state evaluation requirements:** Real "evaluation" in the sense of judgments being made about teachers' suitability is only made in one year of the four-year cycle, the Evaluation year. In the other three years of the cycle, evaluation in the sense of judgment is not being done. The state's requirement that evaluation be done every year really means that some meaningful documentation should appear each year as evidence that teacher performance was attended to by the district. The State of New York will accept the documentation proposed above; that is, this plan meets the state's requirements for "evaluation" every year. But the four-year cycle does real Evaluation (in the sense of judgment about teachers' performance) only once in every four years. The other three years are pure but different structures for professional development. It is important that our teaching staff understand this distinction between what the state is calling for and will accept and what real evalu-

ation in the sense of judgment means.

The group decided that the relationship of the observation, collaborative and individual years was as follows:

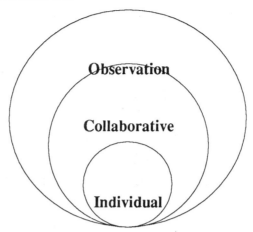

An observational project inherently fulfills the intent and the requirements of a collaborative and an individual project. A collaborative project inherently fulfills the intent and the requirements of an individual project, that is to stimulate individual thinking and growth, but not necessarily the criteria for an observation project. An individual project fulfills the intended requirements for the individual stimulation and learning but not necessarily the criteria for a collaborative or observational project. Observational projects have the most elaborate criteria and are inherently collaborative. Individual projects have the fewest criteria (but, of course, individuals might develop very demanding plans for themselves.)

Therefore, to help people understand the four year cycle and to help them plan activities we will generate a large list of conceivable activities people might do in any year of the four-year cycle. Next to each activity we will write I, C, O or two or three of these letters to signify which year of the cycle a given activity might serve. Therefore, some activities would satisfy the requirement of any year in a three-year cycle, while others would satisfy only the individual year. We will begin constructing this list at our next meeting. It is understood the list will not be exclusive or restrictive of projects teachers might do; that is, teachers might develop projects that are not on the list and yet which still would be acceptable. (See pp. I-195-197.)

STATEMENT TO TEACHERS

In response to New York State's new requirement that a written statement of performance aimed at continuous improvement of instruction be done each year on every teacher, the Professional Growth Committee, comprised of teachers and administrators from all schools, was formed. It designed a pilot plan that would fulfill the State requirement in a manner easy to manage, evaluative in only one of the four years, and beneficial to all concerned. The resultant program would have each tenured teacher evaluated by the administration *one* of the four years in the cycle, and the other three would contain activities which enhanced classroom effectiveness through observation, collaboration and individual choice. Each teacher would enter the sequence, designating which cycle he/she will be emphasizing first and thereby establishing the order that will be followed for the three years. Teachers will design their sequence in conjunction with their building principal in an effort to balance participation and the allocation of resources in each of the component parts of the cycle.

The Professional Growth Committee has recommended that our new professional growth process begin in ___(date)___. While many aspects of the process have been designed, we anticipate that revisions will continue to occur. Therefore, we regard this as a "pilot year."

In this context, "pilot" means that the four year cycle will be implemented and that the Committee will seek honest and candid reactions along with specific suggestions for improvement.

Attached is a detailed description of each of the three non-evaluative years which have been designated as observation, collaboration and individual choice. Also included are forms and formats which will be utilized to fulfill the State's requirement for a "written statement of performance."

In this district each year of its four-year Professional Growth Cycle has a different name signifying the different purposes and activities one may do. The four years are called:

- *the evaluation year*

- *the collaboration year*

- *the observation year*

- *the individual choice year*

Their definitions follow:

COLLABORATION

Definition:
Collaboration is a professional growth experience done with one or more other people for shared reactions during the year.

Criteria:
1. This phase should take place at least once during the four year cycle.
2. The identified goal/focus should contribute to one's professional knowledge and/or skill as a teacher.
3. Activities should take place over an identified period of time.

Sample Activities:
Study group
Working with a consultant toward a common goal
Committee work
Pilot a program
Joint planning of lessons
Grade level or department project
Combinations of the activities

OBSERVATION

Definition:
Observation is defined as a professional growth activity where one's teaching is observed and feedback is given. Its purpose is not to evaluate, but rather to generate communication and useful information about one's teaching.

Criteria:
1. Observations should focus on a particular topic or area.
2. Each observation session should be accompanied by mutual pre-planning and feedback.
3. A written log should be completed after each session by the observed teacher. (Sample log format included.)
4. A minimum of four observations should be made.

Sample Activities:
1. Paired observations—(mutual feedback)
2. One-way observation and feedback (by request and mutual agreement)
3. Video taping (with feedback)
4. Observation by outside consultant
5. Combination of activities

INDIVIDUAL CHOICE

Definition:
Professional growth selected by the teacher and reviewed by the building committee. The activities may or may not involve working with others and should constitute substantial and continuous activity for the year.

Criteria:

1. Activities should take place over an identified period of time.

2. The identified goal/focus should contribute to one's professional knowledge and/or skill as a teacher.

Sample Activities:

1. Course work
2. In-service
3. Workshops
4. Teacher exchange program
5. Independent/self-study
6. Study group (both collaborative and individual)
7. Experimentation within the classroom
8. To choose either of the other two (years) as an option to enhance professional growth
9. Combination of activities.

Artifacts ==

_____ CENTRAL SCHOOL DISTRICT

PROFESSIONAL GROWTH PLAN
for

NAME _____   SCHOOL _____

YEAR _____   CYCLE YEAR* _____

Desired Outcome:

Plan for reaching the desired outcome:

If this is your collaborative or observation year, please indicate the names of people with whom you are working.

☐ If your plan meets the criteria and you would like feedback from the building committee on your plan, please indicate by checking the box.

☐ Check this box if you will be needing resources.

Describe your proposed needs.

SUMMARY OF GROWTH EXPERIENCES

NAME _____

SCHOOL _____   SCHOOL YEAR _____

Summary of Growth Experiences:

(Over)

Assessment of Growth as it relates to your *desired outcomes*.